THE
LIZARD
KING

THE LIZARD KING

The Essential Jim Morrison

JERRY HOPKINS

Collier Books
Macmillan Publishing Company
New York

Maxwell Macmillan International
New York Oxford Singapore Sydney

Published by arrangement with Plexus Publishing Ltd, London

Collier Books
Macmillan Publishing Company
866 Third Avenue
New York, NY 10022

Macmillan Publishing Company is part of the
Maxwell Communication Group of Companies.

Library of Congress Cataloging-in-Publication Data
The lizard king: the essential Jim Morrison/Jerry Hopkins. — 1st
Collier Books trade ed.
        p.   cm.
    ISBN 0-02-020965-7
    1. Morrison, Jim, 1943–1971.   2. Rock musicians—United States—
Biography.
ML420.M62H68   1993
782.42166'092—dc20   93-19987   CIP   MN
[B]

First Collier Books Trade Edition 1993

10   9   8   7   6   5   4   3   2   1

Printed in the United States of America

CONTENTS

INTRODUCTION

I FIRST SAW JIM in 1966 in the London Fog, a small nightclub at the Beverly Hills end of the Sunset Strip in Los Angeles. Despite its classy location, it was a very funky club – not at all like the hangout for the scene-makers who gathered a few blocks away at the Whisky a Go-Go.

It took its name from the fact that it opened during the middle of what was then called an 'invasion' by English rock bands – 'Swinging London' and all of that – so there were British newspapers pasted to the walls. However, there was little else that made you think of London, except for the thick cigarette smoke which could, at a stretch, be thought to resemble London fog. The place smelled of spilled beer and ashtrays. It was dark and very narrow with high ceilings. It appeared as if someone had walled off an alley at both ends. Detroit maybe. Definitely not London.

I remember Jim in unpressed khaki pants and a long-sleeved, pullover cotton shirt, holding onto the hand-mike as if he were about to suck it, while singing some of the raunchiest and most perverse songs I'd heard anywhere. At the time, I was writing a column for *The Los Angeles Free Press*, a weekly underground newspaper, and booking acts for a rock and roll television show called *Shivaree*. This put me on the Sunset Strip four or five nights a week for more than two years, from 1964 to 1966.

Jim was raw, untrained, and obviously ill-at-ease. Frequently he sang with his back to the audience. Nonetheless, there was an undeniable and unavoidable energy - a dark and compelling force. It seemed to me that someone, or several, in the band had read Nietzsche, listened to Brecht and Weil, and taken a lot of LSD.

7

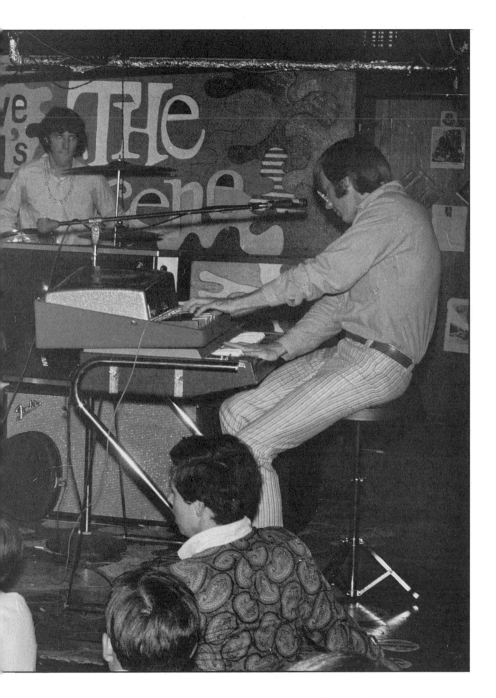

The Doors play The Scene, a tiny but influential blues club in New York.

At the same time, all four of the guys looked like clean-cut university students – which they had been until very recently, although I didn't know it then. Despite this wholesome, collegiate look, the band, and especially Jim, exuded a spooky, Germanic dread. Sexy, but mysterious and threatening. However, the notes I took at the time do not reflect much more than 'group to watch'.

In the years following I did just that. I watched. And then I interviewed Jim, in 1968, and again in 1969, following the obscenity and exposure arrests that virtually destroyed the band. By then they had become one of the most popular groups in the world. I went to Mexico with the Doors for a week, and after that for a year Jim and I got together occasionally. He'd invite me to screenings of his films, or to poetry readings. Sometimes we'd meet in a bar. We weren't friends. It was more like good acquaintances.

A sequence of unimportant but for me significant events began at the time of my second long interview with Jim, an interview for *Rolling Stone*, which turned out to be one of his longest and one of his best; it is included in this book. During one of the interview sessions, Jim asked if we could visit his agent's office, so he could sign a contract for his first book of poetry. We discovered that afternoon that we had the same agent.

I had recently written a small history of rock and roll. Jim said he had read and liked it and he asked what I was planning next. I said I wasn't sure, but the biography intrigued me as a form. I said I was thinking about asking Frank Zappa for his co-operation. Jim merely said, 'I'd like to read a book about Elvis Presley'. The book I later wrote was dedicated to Jim and, coincidentally, the editor who took it was Jim's editor, Jonathan Dolger at Simon & Schuster. By the time the book was published, in 1971, Jim was reported dead in Paris and Jonathan had asked me if I would like to do a book about him. I said yes.

Of course, some regarded this rock singer as little more than another of Hollywood's pretty faces, a flashy, sexy but ultimately inconsequential intellectual street punk and would-be bard who took too much acid and then too much booze, wore tight leather pants, shocked everyone when he sang about fucking his mother, then corked the bottle with a highly publicized arrest for allegedly waving his cock at a crowd of 10,000 in Miami.

But even these most cynical of critics must agree that during his fiery careen through the 1960s, Jim Morrison was a kind of cultural superman, larger than life, moving little girls (and many men) to sexual delight and intellectuals to profundity with equal ease and dispatch. At the same time he was preening and blowing kisses in magazines for sub-teens, the egg-headed New York critic (and Columbia University English professor) Albert Goldman called him a 'surf-born Dionysus' and a 'hippie Adonis'. Posing for early publicity photographs with an obvious erection running down one pantleg, then shifting to a bare-chested look with leather pants, he inspired Digby Diehl (who soon after became the book editor of *The Los Angeles Times*) to describe Jim in an article by referring to Norman O. Brown's 'polymorphous perverse infantile sexuality'. Joan Didion added, 'It was Morrison who wrote most of the Doors lyrics, the peculiar character of which was to reflect either an ambiguous paranoia or a quite unambiguous insistence upon the love-death as the ultimate high.'

At the same time, *Vogue* called him one of the 'ravishing people' and two of the best critics of the period, *Village Voice* columnist Richard Goldstein and *Crawdaddy* editor Paul Williams, effused over him over and over again. There was something there for everyone.

He had modelled his early look from the classics, taking his haircut and the way he held his head from Plutarch's description of Alexander the Great. The curly locks and bunched neck muscles resembled a bust by Michelangelo. Like Brando, when reporters asked him questions, Jim referred them to books, notably Friederich Nietzsche's *The Birth of Tragedy*. He had suits custom-made from the skins of snakes and unborn pony. 'Think of us as erotic politicians,' he told *Newsweek*.

In concert, he resembled the Siberian shaman, rattling his tambourine like a gourd and entering a trance-like state to lead his audience toward communal ecstasy. His lyric themes included insanity, imprisonment, abortion, infanticide, incest and murder. He sang of snakes and drowning horses in a time when other performers sang about wearing flowers in your hair, and getting high with a little help from your friends. Jim urged his fans to push personal boundaries, 'to break on through to the other side'. And he lived on the edge himself, where in true existentialist tradition, he 'woke up' to discover that 'the end is near'. He told a generation starved for love that 'music is your only friend'. He spoke directly to the ache of loneliness. He captured the impatience of a generation that was frustrated and angry about the way things were being run. We heard incredible stories about his catching dragon flies on the wing in his mouth and eating them, and sticking pins into the pupils of his eyes. 'I am the Lizard King,' he said. 'I can do anything!'

We believed it and he came to believe it, too, for a while.

Those who think Jim is alive today do so for a variety of reasons. To begin with, Jim was 'perfect' for immortality, because when he was alive, he died so frequently. When the Doors were at their height in the late 1960s, Jim 'died' in rumour nearly every weekend, usually in a car accident (like James Dean), and often in a fall from a hotel balcony where he'd been showing off for friends, either by hanging from it by his hands, or dancing along its edge. At other times he 'died' from an overdose of something alcoholic, hallucinogenic, or sexual.

The French writer Edgar Morin wrote about the James-Dean-is-alive idea in his book about Hollywood, *The Stars*. He said there was a 'spontaneous naive phenomenon: the refusal to believe in the hero's death. The death of every superman (good or evil) has been doubted and disbelieved, because the faithful were never able to believe these heroic figures were entirely mortal.' So it was with Jim Morrison.

The believers said it was out of character for Jim to die of a heart attack in a bathtub, the 'official' story. Nonetheless, the official story prevailed. Jim's manager, Billy Siddons, was the one who told the story, and he got it from Pamela Courson, who was Jim's girlfriend, or 'common-law wife', as she was

Jim and Robby Krieger take a break between songs.

The Doors on Venice Beach, 1966.

soon described in the press. She told Billy that she was alone with Jim in their Paris flat (sometime after midnight on Friday, July 2nd, 1971) when Jim regurgitated a small quantity of blood. Jim had done that before, she said, and although she was concerned, she was not worried. Jim claimed he felt okay, said he was going to take a bath, and Pamela fell back asleep. At five, she said, she awoke, saw Jim had not returned to the bed, went into the bathroom and found him still in the tub, his arms along the porcelain sides, head back, long wet hair matted against the rim, a boyish smile across his recently clean-shaven face. She thought he was playing one of his jokes. But then the fire department's resuscitation unit was called, and a doctor and police followed. At least that is the way the story went.

One factor causing initial disbelief was timing. Billy Siddons told his (Pamela's) story to the press a full six days after Jim had died, two days after the funeral. 'I have just returned from Paris, where I attended the funeral of Jim Morrison,' Siddons said in a prepared statement (released by a publicity firm in Beverly Hills). 'Jim was buried in a simple ceremony, with only a few friends present. The initial news of his death and funeral was kept quiet because those of us who knew him intimately and loved him as a person wanted to avoid all the notoriety and circus-like atmosphere that surrounded the deaths of such other rock personalities as Janis Joplin and Jimi Hendrix.

'I can say that Jim died peacefully of natural causes – he had been in Paris since March with his wife, Pam. He had seen a doctor in Paris about a respiratory problem and had complained of his problem on Saturday, the day of his death . . . '

In the days that followed, Siddons offered no more information because he had none. He could only guess at what, specifically, had caused the reported heart stoppage, the announced cause of death. (In France, when there is no obvious sign of foul play, autopsies are not required.) Perhaps it was a blood clot moving into his heart from where it had formed when he did one of those famous second-storey dives. Perhaps it was a recurrence of pneumonia, which he'd had less than a year before. Perhaps he merely drank too much. It couldn't have been heroin; everyone agreed: Jim's drug of choice was booze. All Siddons could add was a description of the funeral and cemetery. Jim had walked the cobblestoned streets and dirt paths of the *Cimetière du Père-Lachaise* only a few days before his death, Siddons said, seeking the graves of Colette, Heloise and Abelard, Sarah Bernhardt, Edith Piaf, Oscar Wilde, Honoré de Balzac, Proust, Rossini, Bizet, and Chopin. Siddons said Jim had expressed a wish to be buried there.

'There was no service,' he said, 'and that made it all the better. We just threw some flowers and dirt and said goodbye.'

In the days following, a few more details were learned, but they only added to the confusion and mystery. Rumours had spread quickly from Paris to London and then to the U.S. within two days of the reported death – rumours which were traced back to a disc jockey in a Left Bank discotheque who had announced the death to a stunned Saturday night audience the same day Jim died. Nonetheless, on Wednesday, the day Pamela filed the death certificate at the American Embassy and James Douglas Morrison, identified only as a poet, was lowered into the ground, United Press International reported that Jim was not dead, but 'very tired and resting in an unnamed Paris hospital'. And the mid-week edition of France's popular music trade paper headlined a story, 'Jim Morrison *N'Est Pas Mort* (Jim Morrison Is Not Dead)'.

Why all the denials? Why no public statement from a doctor? Were the police involved, and if not, why not? Why were Pamela's friends in Paris refusing to say anything to anyone? How was it that an American citizen could be buried so quickly and quietly in a famous graveyard like Père-Lachaise? Or was Jim, indeed, still alive in an unnamed Paris hospital? What the hell was going on? Billy Siddons had nothing more to say and Pamela had gone into seclusion, reportedly still in shock.

Time passed and a Jim Morrison cult blossomed. Fan mail and epic poems arrived daily at the Elektra Records and Doors offices. Two grieving fans committed suicide. And from the media came a freshet of tribute, turning into a river of gore, as writers tilted with credibility in creating 'The Curse

*Jim Morrison with Ray Manzarek during a pre-
concert sound check. Manzarek and Morrison
were intellectual equals and worked well together.*

of J'. Now that Brian <u>Jones</u> and <u>Jimi</u> Hendrix and <u>Janis</u> Joplin and <u>Jim</u> Morrison were gone (all at 27!), were not the days also numbered for Mick <u>Jagger</u> and <u>John</u> Lennon and <u>Jerry</u> Garcia, etc? On the street in 1971, such a question was regarded portentously.

Within six months, the posthumous product began to appear. In January, 1972, Elektra issued a two-record anthology of Doors material, packaged with the slogan '22 Classic Doors Songs – Special Low Price'. At the same time in London, someone bootlegged some unreleased jam sessions featuring Jimi and Jim, among others, on an album called *Sky High*, whose cover featured a grinning skull. In April, a radio station in Baltimore conducted a two-hour seance 'live' over the air in an attempt to contact Jim's spirit, and, presumably, energize listener ratings. In June, *Esquire* delivered a bitter and retrospective slap entitled 'The Real-Life Death of Jim Morrison: Slamming the Door on the Woodstock Nation'. And on a slightly less commercial level, when classes resumed at San Diego State University three months after that, one of the new courses was called 'Rock Poetry' and it featured Jim's lyrics and was listed in the university catalogue under 'Comparative Literature'. At the same time in Los Angeles, a Jim Morrison Film Fund of $40,000 was announced at UCLA, where Jim had been a cinematography student. And, in November, readers of *Playboy* magazine elected Jim to the *Playboy* Jazz & Pop Hall of Fame.

Simultaneously in Paris, the Doors' final album, *L.A. Woman*, was awarded the Grand Prize of the Academie Charles Cros – the 'Grammy' of the French music industry – and was named Album of the Year by the readers of France's most articulate pop music magazine, *Rock & Fol*k. In the same poll, Jim also was named France's No. 1 *chanteur* – though he was not French, and never had sung publicly in France.

The worshipful infatuation reached a kind of peak in France a year later when on May 1st 1973, the remaining three Doors performed at the Olympia Theatre in Paris to one of the group's most emotional audiences. I happened to be in Europe that year, as a correspondent for *Rolling Stone*, and I flew to Paris for the concert. There were many in the 2,000-

seat theatre who were in tears, and many who wondered why no one in the band even so much as mentioned Jim that night, or visited the grave the next day. The Doors did not do so, they said later, fearing an unpleasant crowd scene.

At the cemetery there was a crowd, Doors or no Doors. Within days of Jim's burial, his grave became a pilgrimage site. 'Flower bower' is what the *Manchester Guardian* called it, while in France *L'Express* termed it 'la grand migration' and *The Los Angeles Times* headlined its story 'Daily Mini Music Festival at Jim Morrison's Grave'. Only a hand-lettered plaque on a temporary wooden stand marked the plot, but the grave was unmistakably that of France's No. 1 *chanteur*. Jim's fans had spray-painted arrows on tombs showing the way to the site, and once there, the visitor found graffiti in French, German, Spanish, and English covering all the nearby head-stones and sepulchres. The plot itself was so small it seemed as if Jim might have been buried standing up. Around it was a border of scallop shells and near the plaque there were bunch-es of flowers, collages and paintings, and poems streaked with recent rain. Standing and sitting nearby were young European and American fans, smoking cigarettes, playing guitars, whis-pering in reverent tones, offering toasts to the dead singer with bottles of beer and cheap wine.

Perhaps even more interesting than the physical evidence of a cult were the theories being developed about how, and why, Jim died, or didn't die. The Parisians held out for heroin as the cause of death. After all, they said, hadn't that disc jock-ey, an American exile named Cameron Watson, got his infor-mation the very day Jim died from a known junkie, who had told the same disc jockey a few days earlier that he was buy-ing 3,000 francs ($500) worth of smack for Jim and Marianne Faithfull? This, at least, is what Watson told me and presum-ably told many others. And didn't some of the graffiti at *Père-Lachaise* – 'Have mercy for junkies' and *'shootez'* – support the theory that it was a drug overdose and not a heart attack? And wasn't Jim found in a bathtub, usually the first place a victim of an overdose is taken for attempted revival?

One of New York's young, flashy entertainment lawyers of the time, Richard Golub, had an even juicier theory. He called

*Jim modelling Gloria Stavers' fur coat during a
photo session in her New York apartment.*

me at my office at *Rolling Stone* in London. We met at a nearby pub, where he told me, unequivocally, that Jim was murdered. Golub based his claim largely on an interview with a French model and actress, Elizabeth (ZoZo) Larivière, from whom Jim and Pamela subleased their Paris flat. She was quoted as saying that a door between the living room and one of the bedrooms had been broken open, the lock and knob removed. Golub said she found a bloody tee-shirt in the closet, a bloody knife under the bed. She also gave Golub a carton of papers, tapes and notebooks that had been left behind, including several threatening letters from someone who claimed to be Jim's ex-wife and who on the basis of even the most superficial examination of the letters appeared to be disturbed. Golub wanted to sell me (*Rolling Stone*) the story and the box of stuff. I declined.

The most bizarre theory had Jim the victim of a political conspiracy aimed at discrediting and eliminating the hippie/New Left/counter-culture lifestyle – a vast, pervasive and, according to the initiates, connected set of conspiracies that also included the shootings at Kent State and Jackson State, the riots at Isla Vista, the Weatherman bombings, the stiff prison sentences given Timothy Leary and the Chicago Eight, the Charlie Manson murders, and the deaths of Brian Jones, Janis Joplin, Jimi Hendrix and more than two dozen Black Panthers.

There were others who believed that Jim had overdosed on cocaine, a drug he was known to enjoy. While still more merely shrugged and said that forgetting the murder stories, it didn't matter precisely how Jim died – whether he overdosed on something, had a heart attack caused by a blood clot or respiratory failure, or merely drank himself to death (as so many had surmised from the start) – the bottom line still read 'suicide'. One way or another, he was dead of self-abuse, however slow or fast, and finding out how was merely a matter of determining the calibre of the metaphorical pistol he had held to his head.

On the other hand, there were those who wouldn't buy any of this. The easiest thing to get going in the preparation of *No One Here Gets Out Alive* was a conversation about the possibility that Jim Morrison was not dead and buried in that famous cemetery in Paris. Practically everyone I talked to while researching my book asked if I was certain that he was dead. At the Olympia Theatre the night the surviving Doors performed, members of the audience cried out, 'Jim . . . are you here?'

This was not a fantasy without circumstantial support. Clearly there was believable motivation: by faking his death, the thinking went, Jim was merely seeking the peace he couldn't find as a rock star and sex idol. During his life, he sought credibility as a poet and so had done nothing more at the so-called end of it than disappear from view in order to have the time to write and, with his disappearance, gain the freedom that anonymity brings.

There were several instances when the seeds of such a possible hoax were sown – at the Fillmore Auditorium in San Francisco in 1967, when the Doors still hadn't had a hit record and Jim suggested pulling a death stunt for the publicity it would bring . . . in his telling me, among others, that he could see himself changing careers radically, reappearing as a suited and neck-tied business executive . . . in the plot-line of a film script he planned with a Hollywood screenwriter shortly before going to Paris, which had the protagonist abandoning his family in Los Angeles to disappear into the Mexican jungle in search of what Jim called 'absolute zero . . . in the concept of a show conceived with a classical composer, also just before he went to Paris, which had as its hero a returning Vietnam prisoner-of-war, someone who'd virtually been dead for years, returning to his old scene with 'new eyes' . . . and in the life-line of a French poet Jim admired and was much influenced by, Arthur Rimbaud, who after writing all his poetry by the age of 19, disappeared into North Africa to become a gun runner and slave trader. In support of such speculation, many of Jim's closest friends agreed it was the sort of stunt Jim would attempt, and with Pamela's cooperation, could actually pull off.

Of course I wanted to interview Pam and after more than a year of patient pursuit, she agreed to have lunch with me at a

Jim in action at the Fillmore East.

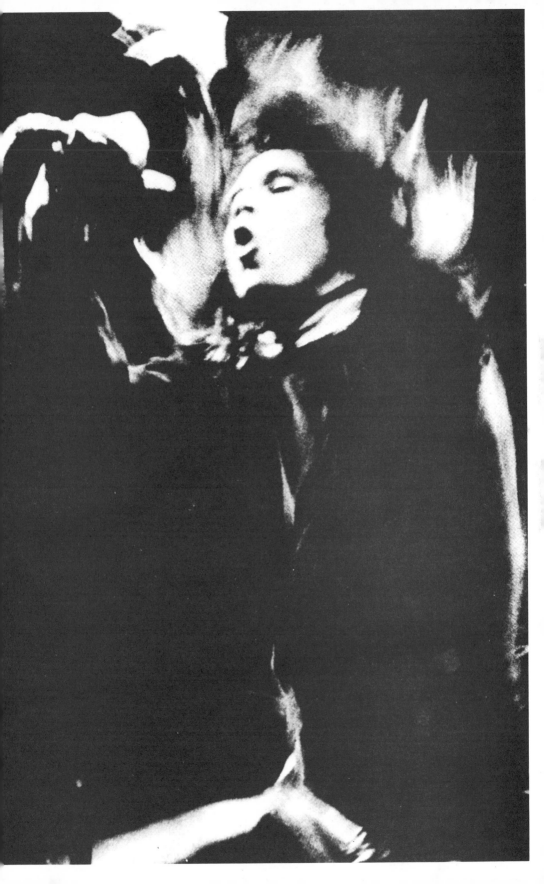

fashionable restaurant in Beverly Hills. When Jim was alive, I hadn't seen much of Pam and, like so many others, I underestimated her role in Jim's life, thinking she was more a pretty trinket than a soul mate, as Jim frequently said in his songs. So I wasn't prepared for how protective she was. Nor was I prepared for her striking beauty. That trendy restaurant where we met was known as a hangout for the Hollywood crowd and Pamela fitted right in. She was thin and curvy and her auburn hair and pale skin dusted with freckles gave her a delicacy and fragility that made you want to take care of her. (A key part of understanding Jim and Pam's relationship, by the way; from all I could determine later, part of Jim's attraction to her was rooted in her apparent dependency.)

Pamela told me that Jim had liked the way I wrote about the Doors for *Rolling Stone*. She quoted him as saying I had been fair, I wasn't like all the rest, who made him look like such a jerk. If Pamela was manipulating me, trying to disarm me, it worked.

At the time, she was fighting to collect Jim's legacy. Jim left a will and in it he gave virtually everything to Pamela, what little cash was on hand, and one-quarter of the Doors' future earnings. But the surviving members of the group filed suit, saying Jim had pulled more than his share out of the communal bank account before he died, so until that was accounted for and settled, Pamela's portion was held in escrow.

We spent two hours together and I learned only a little about Jim's life and nothing about his death. And not long after that, Pamela was herself dead of a heroin overdose. Later I was told on good authority that she had been selling her fragile beauty by the hour for nearly two years and that her pimp had been one of Jim's so-called friends and one-time chauffeur.

At the lunch, Pamela asked me why I wanted to write a book about Jim. 'When Jim died,' I said, 'it affected me more than I thought our relationship warranted. I want to know why.'

Jim Morrison at Winterland in San Francisco.
Morrison's stage presence was one of his greatest
assets as a performer.

In retrospect, that sort of makes me sound like a Jim Morrison groupie, which I don't think I am. It also sounds shallow, which I hope I'm not. But Morrison had touched me, and I was curious. I think I expected to find all my answers in researching and writing the book. I was wrong, of course. Thus, this second book.

But first, a few words about *No One Here Gets Out Alive*.

The manuscript I submitted to Simon & Schuster was about the size of the Manhattan telephone directory and my editor asked that I cut it down. By the time I did that, the editor figured Jim's time had come and gone in the book market and the second, much smaller manuscript was rejected. Over the next six years, another 30 or so publishers also rejected the book. Finally, in December 1977, I sent copies of the manuscript to five London publishers. When they added their names to the list of rejections, I gave up.

Danny Sugerman is a young man – not so young any more, I guess – who <u>was</u> a Doors groupie. He worshipped Jim Morrison when he was alive and from the moment of Jim's death or disappearance, he devoted all his life to keeping Jim's memory alive and well polished. I interviewed him while doing research for the book. We stayed in touch and when 1978 rolled around and I had those 30-plus rejections, I figured the hell with it, I'd given Morrison enough of my time for this lifetime, and I told Danny so. He said he wanted to try to sell the book and I said sure, go ahead, find a publisher and you've got 10 per cent.

Danny sent the large version of the manuscript to Warner Books, not knowing that Warner had rejected the manuscript twice – once when it went in cold, the second time when I imposed on a friend and got it onto the desk of the company president, who wrote me a one-line letter: 'We're still not interested.' Fortunately, this time the manuscript went not to the president's office, but to that of a young woman who said she wanted to publish the book.

Jim Morrison at Bill Graham's Fillmore East.
Morrison knew how to use a microphone for both
vocal and sexual effect.

*Jim and Pamela posing in the high-class hippy
clothes she sold in the shop he bought her.*

When she took her recommendation to the editorial board, she was told no, the book had been rejected twice and that was it. She was young, but she had brought in several bestsellers since joining the company and finally the others agreed to publish the book, so long as Hopkins and Sugerman didn't get anything much in advance. We happily accepted $1,500 and soon after that Danny asked if he could merge the two manuscripts to create a third. I said yes. We spent the $1,500 on a typist.

Danny says now that he and Ray Manzarek, the Doors' keyboardist, who was paying Danny's room and board at the time, edited out a lot of the more unsavoury anecdotes. I don't know, maybe they did. But I do know that the final manuscript was better than Manuscripts One and Two. Danny also wrote an introduction, got the poet Michael McClure (a friend of Jim's) to write an Afterword, helped round up the photographs, and handled the problem of the dual endings.

When I first wrote the book, I had two endings. In the first ending, Jim died of an overdose of heroin and alcohol. In the second ending, Jim faked his death and disappeared. It was my notion that if the publisher printed 10,000 copies of the book, half would end with the overdose, the other half would end with the disappearance, and the books would be distributed randomly, with no one saying a thing. I thought it was an interesting concept – I still do – and I thought it fitted Jim's psychology. Besides, I really didn't know how he died.

The publisher rejected the concept and suggested the two endings be blended into a single, ambiguous chapter, which Danny did (thereby accomplishing the same purpose in fewer words and avoiding a distribution nightmare). I guess that fanned the flames of the cult.

No One Here Gets Out Alive was published in the United States in June 1980, went right onto all the bestseller lists and straight up to No. 1. It remained on those lists for nine months and as I write this, it is still selling. It has sold consistently for more than ten years and, at the time of writing, is back on international bestseller lists. So far, more than 5 million copies are in print and the book has been published in about a dozen other countries, from Greece to Japan to Mexico.

It is now 1992 and a lot has gone under the musical bridge. During that time, I've learned much new about Jim. In fact, at one point I wanted to write a second book about Jim and Pam, a love story. I started re-interviewing some of my earlier sources. But I couldn't get a publisher interested.

There are two parts to this second book. The first is a brief retelling of Jim's life. In it, I go over some familiar territory, but also add a lot of information – and interview material – that was left out of the first book, as well as put in stuff I've learned since the first book was published. This is not revisionist biography, designed to replace *No One Here Gets Out Alive*, but is another run past the myth, another attempt to capture, and perhaps get closer to explaining, the mystery and mystique. And it tells what happened during Jim's final days in Paris.

The second part of this book is pure, unadulterated Jim, in his own words – a select collection of Question-and-Answer interviews that were conducted during Jim's brief career. My own interview for *Rolling Stone* is included.

Jim Morrison was one of the most intelligent and articulate performers I've ever met. Most rock performers aren't even articulate as rock performers. Jim was that – in spades. His lyrics still work today. More than that, Jim was able to express himself, and his ideas, in conversation.

What follows may seem familiar. I will hit the biographical benchmarks which are necessary, and I will tell some familiar stories, because they are too important to leave aside. However, a lot of what follows is new. That is, it never before has been published, nor anywhere else is likely to be.

THE
BIOGRAPHY

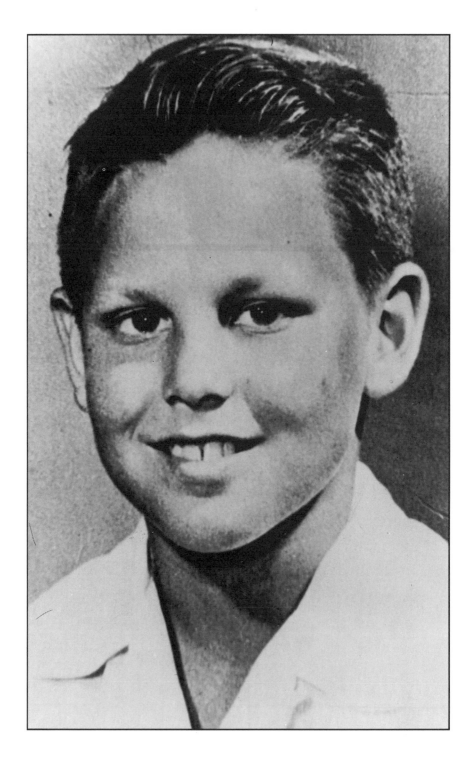

I

The Child

JIM'S FATHER, Steve, was from Leesburg, Florida, and when he was in high school in the 1930s he was too small for football, so he was a cheerleader and a gymnast. He got good grades and was a gentleman. 'We didn't dare do anything we weren't supposed to do,' said Fran Warfield, who went to school with Steve. 'We behaved ourselves. That was the way Steve was all his life. He was a leader, but he was military all the way, he toed the line.'

Steve met Jim's mother Clara Clarke in Honolulu in 1941, soon after he graduated from the U.S. Naval Academy. In many ways, she was Steve's opposite. She was as blonde as he was dark and the daughter of a maverick lawyer in Wisconsin who had run for political office as a Communist. Clara even lived in a commune as a child; once, her family traded a dog for a tyre to get back to Wisconsin. Friends from the period when Clara was in Hawaii describe her as a goodtime party girl, with a somewhat domineering personality. She met Steve Morrison at a military dance shortly before Pearl Harbor was attacked by the Japanese, in 1941.

They married soon after and together they went to Florida, where Steve learned to fly before being assigned to an aircraft carrier in the Pacific. Jim was born on December 8th, 1943, in Melbourne, near what is now Cape Kennedy. For the next two years, until the war ended, he and his mother lived with his father's parents in Clearwater, in a house whose wide green lawn sloped down to the Gulf of Mexico. His grandparents, Paul and Caroline Morrison, were teetotallers and church-goers. They ran a small laundry in town. It was a safe, warm growing-up environment, but for Clara, fairly dull.

When Steve Morrison returned following the end of the

war, he and his family began a typical military lifestyle, moving frequently because of his assignments. Jim acquired a sister, Anne, and then a brother, Andy. They lived in Albuquerque, New Mexico, and then in Los Altos, California, then briefly in Washington, D.C., returning again to California, to Claremont near Los Angeles.

At the age of five, Jim was in a car travelling along a highway between Albuquerque and Santa Fe with his father and his grandmother Caroline. She told me, 'We came upon an accident. Indians were wailing and crying. Later, we thought that was very unusual, because we thought Indians didn't cry. We thought they were more stoic than that. Jimmy was very much affected. He wanted to do something. We stopped and then we went on to call the highway police and an ambulance. Jimmy wanted to do more. He was so upset, his father finally had to say, "Jimmy, you dreamed it. It didn't happen. It's not true, you just had a bad dream."'

Years later, Jim would claim that the souls of those dying Indians leaped into his head when the Morrison car stopped. It was a good thing to say, in the sixties. Hippies had made native Americans a part of their 'thing'. After all, after breaking camp, didn't Indians leave the earth as they'd found it? And, like so much Jim said to the press, it was so eminently quotable. Souls from dying Indians leaping into a future rock star's head? What an image. No wonder, when Oliver Stone made his movie, this would become the first scene, providing the theme for Jim's life – a modern-day shaman.

'The shaman,' Oliver told me, 'that's my hook.'

Jim's dad's assignment in Albuquerque had something to do with the atomic bomb. Steve was assigned to White Sands. It was all top secret and Jim's parents made a pact not to talk about his work at home, an agreement that remained in force for many years. Steve's cousin Thad Morrison told me that Jim ultimately came to resent the alienation that resulted from the long absences and the secrecy: 'I think the ultimate break between Jim and his father was over Steve's putting the Navy ahead of the family, which is what you had to do when you were an officer.'

According to Jim's brother Andy, it was the quasi-military

Rear Admiral George S. Morrison

way of disciplining the children that solidified the separation. Their parents had decided never to punish the children physically, but to find another way. The way they picked was to 'dress them down' (a military phrase), to tell them what they had done wrong over and over again, until reducing them to tears. Andy told me that he always cried, but Jim learned to hold tears back. Today, such practices are generally regarded as emotional abuse, which can in their way be as damaging as physical punishment.

Jim's high school years started in 1957 in Alameda, California, a small island in San Francisco Bay known for its large Navy air station. Commander Morrison was now a flight deck officer aboard the *USS Midway*, an aircraft carrier. Jim was fourteen and this was his seventh home town.

His best friend was named Fud Ford. They did everything together. They made fools of themselves at the Navy officers' club to embarrass Jim's parents' friends. They sneaked their first drinks from a bottle of gin at Jim's house and replaced what they drank with water. They raised hell in the local movie theatre and staged practical jokes at school. They found a way to sneak into a female classmate's boathouse to watch her change into her swim suit. It was, basically, normal teenage stuff.

More unusual was Jim's interest in writing and art, where the subject usually was sexual or scatological. Fud saved many examples. There were mock radio commercials about masturbation. One of Jim's most extreme pencil drawings showed a man with a Coca Cola bottle for a penis, a can opener for testicles, slime running from his anus. Another drawing showed a Navy officer in one of those Gilbert & Sullivan coats and hats, dripping with braid, the officer looking cross-eyed, and drooling.

Jim also clipped comic strip characters from the Sunday funny papers, pasted them in new configurations and wrote new dialogue. They, too, showed Jim's adolescent fascination with sex and defecation. They also demonstrated a sophistication well beyond his age.

In one of them, one of Donald Duck's nephews was shown looking closely at Pluto's rear end. Li'l Lulu was approaching, her mouth wide open, her hands held out in front of her, as if upset. She is saying, 'Just what do you think you're doing to my dog?' The duck replies 'My dear young woman, do you realize this dog has one of the finest assholes I have ever seen!'

In another, Dennis the Menace says to Nancy (of *Nancy and Sluggo*), 'What did I do? What did I say? I thought you found my sexual affection stimulating.' Nancy is pictured running away, saying, 'Don't sweat it, man, I'm going down to the drug store for a small purchase.'

In a third, Lucy tells Charlie Brown, 'I'll give you 50 cents if you'll fuck me, Charlie Brown,' and he says, looking very bored, 'Throw in your trycicle [sic] and it's a deal, Baby.'

Fud told me that he couldn't cut out the characters fast enough to keep up with Jim's facile mind.

Halfway through his sophomore year, the Morrisons moved again, this time into a big house in what was called 'the Beverly Hills' of Alexandria, Virginia, where Jim enrolled in George Washington High School, a segregated school whose student body reflected the surrounding upper-middle class, white Anglo-Saxon population. The Commander was now at the Pentagon.

One of the best interviews I got while researching the book came out of a weekend I spent with Jim's brother Andy, who was five years younger than Jim. He remembered Jim's high school years in detail, but not entirely happily. He said Jim tormented him constantly. Once, Jim taped Andy's mouth shut as he slept, because Andy's asthma was causing him to make too much noise.

'He'd pick up a rock and say, "I'll give you 10." You said, "No, wait a minute, no, no . . . " And he'd say, "One . . . " And you'd start to run and he'd say, "Fourfivesixseven-eightnineten!" and clobber you. Another time he came at me with one of those plastic dog shits, holding it in his hand in a towel. He chased me all over the house and finally caught me and ground it into my face and it was . . . rubber. And you're expecting something smelly, sticky, and warm. He'd reach over when he was walking with me and somebody else and he'd grab the other guy and say, "Hey . . . my brother wants to fight you . . . mah bruther wonts tew faht chewwww, so what

*Jim aged 16, in a school photo taken in 1961
when he was a pupil at George Washington High
School, Virginia.*

are you gonna do about it?" He'd turn your words back on you and make you look stupid. "Hey, man, what'd you climb that tree for?" I'd read in the paper that morning about the man climbing Everest and said, "Because it was there." And he said, "Yeah, but that pile of dogshit is there, are you gonna eat it?" What do you say to that? If you get on the defensive, that's it with Jim, you're dead.'

Jim also tormented his girlfriend, Tandy Martin, who lived in a house nearby. On a bus trip to Washington, D.C., Jim pulled off Tandy's shoes and socks and exclaimed, so everyone on the bus could hear, 'I want to kiss your precious feet!' More than once, in Washington, Jim told her, 'Find your own way home,' then he ran away. 'I'd have no idea where I was,' she told me. 'I'd have no idea how to get home and I'd start wailing: "Jim, Jim, no, please don't leave me." And he'd come back, laughing.'

As they walked to and from school together, Jim said things to shock and embarrass Tandy: 'You know what I'm gonna do? I'm gonna go over there and piss on that fireplug.' Another time, he taunted her into kissing a statue's backside, keeping it up until she lost her temper and screamed at him, by which time he was standing some distance away and everyone in the park was staring at her. Once, when he saw a paraplegic in a wheelchair, he started mocking him. He used four-letter words in front of Tandy's mother. At night, he stood outside her house and stared at her bedroom window.

In school, he walked up to female students he didn't know, bowed deeply, and recited romantic, eighteenth century poetry. Once in class, he ran around the room, chasing an imaginary bee. He left another class, saying he had to go home because he was having brain surgery that afternoon.

Tandy asked him why he always played such games. He said, 'You'd never stay interested in me if I didn't.'

Tandy thought she wanted to be an actress. She said Jim admired her for that, because he wanted to be in a play, but didn't have the nerve to get up on a stage. He also declined to join a fraternity. 'When you're in high school and you're dif-ferent,' she said, 'like, I wanted to join a sorority because I wanted to be "in", but I knew it was bullshit, so I couldn't do it. I got bid to the top sorority and I went home and cried all night because I knew I'd have to say no. I was emotionally damaged. When you think that you're right and everybody else is doing something else and you're only fifteen years old, well, what happens is: your heart breaks. And a scar forms. Everybody wants to belong when they're fifteen. Jim was asked to join AVO – the fraternity – and he said no.'

Jim's room was in the basement. This gave him his own private entrance, allowing him to leave for school in the morning without being seen, so his mother couldn't say anything about the fact that he was wearing the same shirt for the fifth day in a row. It also gave him a refuge away from the rest of the family, where he spent most of his spare time alone. He had his own refrigerator, where he sometimes kept beer and wine.

He painted, turning out copies of DeKooning nudes, self-portraits, and impressionist paintings of friends, and then he painted over them. He filled up notebooks with poems. Some of them survived, becoming songs years later when he sang with the Doors. One was about horses being jettisoned from sailing ships becalmed in the Sargasso Sea. Tandy remembered a line from a poem he wrote for her: 'But one/The most beautiful of all/Dances in a ring of fire/And throws off the challenge with a shrug.'

Jim's bedroom was walled with books, on shelves he built himself. While in Alameda he was struck by Jack Kerouac's novel *On the Road* and since then read all the beat generation poets and novelists and had their books lined up next to books by Balzac, Rimbaud, Molière, Joyce, Camus, and Baudelaire. It was a good list for a sixteen-year-old. Even his teachers were impressed.

Deucalion Gregory was Jim's English teacher. He said, 'Jim read as much and probably more than any other student in class. His work was excellent. But everything he read was so completely off-beat. I had another teacher who was going to the Library of Congress to check to see if the books Jim was reporting on actually existed or he was making it up. English books on sixteenth and seventeenth century demonology. I've never heard of them, but they existed, and I'm convinced from the paper he wrote that he read them, and if he read

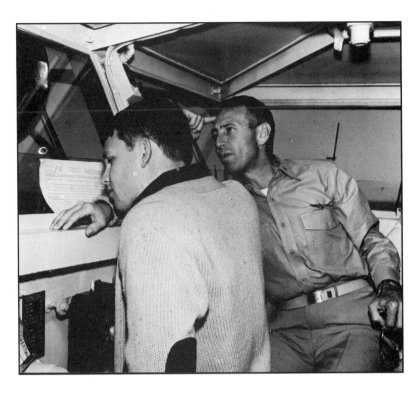

Jim and his father on the bridge of the USS Bon
Homme Richard *in January 1964.*

them, the Library of Congress would've been the only source. Other kids were reading authors represented in our anthology, and Jim was reading Burton's studies of Arab sexuality, which I didn't even know were in print. He read that kind of book, and handled it beautifully in his written work.'

Jim's grades were good, but not exceptional. His scholastic average was 88.32, a high B. Andy told me that Jim once hollered at his parents, 'Hey, you know, the only reason you want me to get good grades is so you can go to your bridge club and brag about it!' I.Q. tests administered during his senior year indicated exceptional intelligence, with a quotient of 149. As close as he was to genius, it appeared that while Jim took on intellectual challenges well beyond his peers, he really didn't care about grades enough to work at them. This is common among the highly intelligent. Jim also refused to attend his graduation ceremony, a source of great embarrassment to his parents.

II

THE SCHOLAR

AT THE END of the school year, Jim was packed off to Clearwater, Florida, to live with his Grandfather Paul and Grandmother Caroline Morrison. Jim's father had kept his parents' home as his 'permanent' address and that made it cheaper for Jim to attend a state school, so for the next year during the day, Jim attended classes at St. Petersburg Junior College; in the evenings and on weekends, he harassed his grandparents. His grandmother said he never let up. They were still non-drinkers, so Jim enjoyed letting them find empty wine bottles in his bedroom trash basket, and frequently came home drunk late at night. He scoffed at their notions of personal hygiene, refusing to shave, get a haircut, or change his clothes. He shocked them at every opportunity, frequently threatening to bring home his 'nigger girlfriend'.

He spent his afternoons at a coffee shop whose owner was a known homosexual. This man told Jim that when he went cruising for guys, he always went without underwear, saying, 'Always show your meat,' advice that, years later, would serve Jim well as a rock star.

Jim refused to go to church.

After registering for the draft, he got excessively drunk. An uncle who lived in Clearwater was obliged to get him out of a situation so sticky that 30 years later, as I was doing my interviews, no one would talk about it.

Grandmother Caroline told me that Jim never shared anything in his life. He wouldn't talk about his school, his friends, his interests, or his plans for the future. Sometimes, she said, he would read something from one of the notebooks he was keeping, but it always was something aimed at shocking her and her husband. 'He was mannerly,' she said, 'but queer.'

It must have been a relief for the elder Morrisons when, in September 1961, Jim started classes at Florida State University, several hours' drive away, in Tallahassee, the state capital. Jim remained at FSU for only a year, but he made a lasting impression. He majored in theatre arts and a fellow student, Keith Carlson, remembered what it was like working with Jim in a play, *The Dumbwaiter*.

'Every night waiting for the curtain to go up, I had no idea what he was going to do. He was difficult to key on, because he tended to play the role very differently all the time. He wasn't keying on me, or on dialogue, or on any of the traditional things. He played scenes and delivered lines with an inflection that seemed totally unmotivated, or at least unexpected. There was a constant undercurrent of apprehension, a feeling that things were on the brink of lost control. Back in those days [1963], everyone was uptight about any obscenity on stage, but we had some wonderfully obscene rehearsals. There was no obscenity during any of the performances, but with Jim, we just never knew.'

Chris Kallivokas knew Jim from Clearwater and roomed with him at FSU. He said Jim was a troublemaker, always looking for a reaction. He gave bus drivers a $20 bill, then gave them a hard time when they didn't have change. When his roommates were taking up a collection to pay the electric bill, Jim refused to contribute because he had an electric blanket, forcing them to freeze. They cut the cord to his blanket in retaliation.

When his roommates insisted he wear a tie to a party, he tied it so that the knot was the 'size of a grapefruit with a tie about three inches under it'. When someone at the party said he liked Jim's knot, Jim said, 'You like my <u>nuts</u>? You crave my body?' and he bit the guy's date on the neck and recited something from Dante's *Inferno*.

'Sometimes he wore small Five & Dime Ben Franklin glasses,' Chris said. 'In 1962 Jim looked like what college kids looked like in 1968.'

Kallivokas said Jim's exhibitionist tendencies were well developed. He urinated in a public fountain in front of a theatre just after the movie ended and the audience was filing past. Walking across campus, he shoved his hands down into the front of his pants when co-eds approached. He whistled at secretaries in downtown Tallahassee, but only gave half the whistle, and when they turned around, curious, he'd snap his fingers in front of his crotch and laugh. When young girls came to the door at Halloween, Jim greeted them wearing only a West Point robe he had picked up somewhere. Then, after giving them candy, he propositioned the trick-or-treaters and opened his robe.

His housemates didn't really think that he would have done anything to those young girls. Nor did they believe him when he said he had let women urinate on a glass coffee table with him lying underneath. They knew it was all for effect. Nonetheless, eventually his roommates told him to leave and Jim packed up his one suitcase of clothing and personal effects and two footlockers of books and moved into a half-trailer with a tar paper roof behind a girls' boardinghouse. Jim later moved into a run-down hotel that once had been home for the prostitutes who serviced the state legislators. The girls had long departed, but the reputation remained, and Jim loved it.

Jim is also remembered in Florida for his intellectual prowess and braggadocio. Several classmates talked about how Jim would wave his arm around his room full of books and ask them to pick one at random and start reading anywhere. Before they had completed a paragraph, Jim identified the book and its author.

For a class in 'Collective Behaviour: The Psychology of Crowds', Jim developed a theory whereby he said he could diagnose and treat a crowd according to its sexual neurosis; his professor was ecstatic, although he was unable to convince his classmates to join him at a college concert to test the theory.

Another professor permitted Jim to choose his own subject for a paper. He chose Hieronymus Bosch, a Dutch artist who considered the world as a kind of hell in which we pass through the Devil's digestive system. Virtually nothing was known then or is known today about Bosch. One of Jim's classmates remembered that 'Jim was fascinated by the gory aspects of the Black Plague and its long-range psychological implications, how it affected the minds of Europeans, affecting the traditions, colouring the climate in which Bosch grew up.' This was bizarre stuff for a college freshman and his history professor was enthralled.

Jim made a lasting impression in every class. Ten years later, the professor who taught Jim the principles of stage design still had three of Jim's watercolours in a trunk in his office. One of these called for a nude male to be hung over the stage. Another, for Tennessee Williams' *Cat on a Hot Tin Roof*, started with a tiny spot of light on the back wall, which grew as the play progressed until it covered the entire set and was revealed as a slide of a cancer cell – recognition of the fact that one of the major characters in the play, Big Daddy, dies of cancer.

Jim was now experimenting with alcohol and, typically, treating it in the same way he treated anything else of interest: compulsively, excessively, dangerously. Once, he borrowed a roommate's T-bird and ran it into a telephone pole. Another time, when some friends began to duel with umbrellas, Jim reached into a police car and stole a policeman's umbrella. The umbrella got lost in the scuffle that followed and Jim was jailed on charges of petty larceny, disturbing the peace, resisting arrest, and public drunkenness. The professor for whom he had written the paper on Bosch bailed him out after he'd spent a night in jail and he had to call home for money to pay a $100 fine.

Jim saw his parents in California only twice during the eighteen months he was at FSU. The first time came at the end of the first year, when he hitchhiked across the country with Bryan Gates, a former housemate. According to Bryan they drank in bars everywhere they stopped, looking for the places Jack Kerouac and his friends had visited in *On the Road*, in New Orleans and Juarez. Always, Bryan said, Jim wanted to take the risky road, to go home with a woman who picked them up in Texas, to visit a whorehouse in Mexico.

Even as a high school student, Jim Morrison
struck staff and fellow students as either brilliant
or weird.

The time at home was short. It was marked by his mother's insistence that he get a haircut and his teaching his brother Andy, then fourteen, dirty jokes which Andy then innocently told his sister and mother, much to Jim's delight. ('What did the blind man say when he passed the fish store?' 'Hello, girls.') Jim then went with Bryan to Los Angeles, where they looked for three weeks for summer jobs, after which Jim was ordered by his mother to return to Coronado to meet his father, whose ship had docked. Jim argued to remain in California, to start school at UCLA in the fall, but after a few days, he was put on a plane and sent back to Florida for an abbreviated summer term. In the fall, he began his sophomore year.

The second visit home came at Christmas, when again his mother insisted he get a haircut before meeting his father, who was now captain of the *USS Bon Homme Richard*, one of the Navy's newest and largest aircraft carriers. Jim's dark hair was almost as short as the captain's and he was wearing khaki slacks and a long-sleeved sweater with leather elbow patches, looking very much like an Ivy League student. He went aboard the carrier and was escorted to the deck so his father could introduce him to the other officers. Later he told friends that his father insisted he fire a machine gun at dummies floating in the water below. Photographs taken at the time imply a strained reunion.

However, a week later Jim finally realized his dream and was enrolled in the 'motion picture division' of the Department of Theatre Arts at UCLA. Later this period would be called the film school's 'Golden Age'. The faculty included three fine directors – Stanley Kramer, Jean Renoir, and Josef Von Sternberg – and the small and eccentric student body included the young Francis Ford Coppola, who was a couple of years ahead of Jim.

Quickly, Jim gathered around him a coterie of neurotic and obsessive odd ducks. Dennis Jakob was called 'The Weasel' or 'The Rat' for his hunched-over, scampering walk. Jim loved him because, he said, Dennis was the only person in the world he had met who had read more books than he had. Dennis and Jim talked endlessly about Frederich Nietzsche. They both identified with Dionysus, 'who was without any images, himself primordial pain and its primordial re-echoing'. It was a phrase they both knew, a philosophical outlook they shared.

John DeBella was the tall, well-muscled son of a New York cop who liked to brag that he had stolen almost as many books as Dennis had read. (He had a long coat with dozens of pockets sewn inside.) John had an almost pathological verbal facility that seemed rooted in Catholic doctrine. He shared with Jim his 'Theory of the True Rumour,' which insisted that perception was everything – to hell with the truth, it was what people believed that was important. ('I am the Lizard King,' Jim would say, years later. 'I can do anything!')

Phil Oleno was the only one in the clique who still lived at home, the source of much teasing from Jim. He looked like a large version of Jim, dark and attractive. Jim was drawn to him because of his obsessive interest in the writings of Carl Jung, who had been a disciple of Freud. Jim preferred another disciple, Sandor Firenczi, who argued for free love. Phil and Jim debated constantly. Phil's father was a pharmacist and that gave him access to drugs, another attraction.

At 34, Felix Venable was the oldest student in the film school, accepted because of the challenge his grades at UC Berkeley presented: they were split equally between As and Fs. He was a wiry guy with a sharp nose and drawn face who reminded Jim of Kerouac's Dean Moriarty, an older guy engaged in a last attempt to bring himself together, frequently stoned on amphetamines, dead before he got his degree.

These four formed Jim's cadre of thrill and perversity, comprised of intelligence, off-beatness, and dare. The year that followed was an extension of Jim's life at FSU: the young beatnik at war with art. It was 1964, the year the Beatles conquered America, running into 1965, when California replied with the Beach Boys and Sonny and Cher. This was the soundtrack to the movie that Jim and his cohorts lived.

The scenes developed immediately. Jim became known for his pungent graffiti in the men's room in the student editing building. He frequented the Lucky U, a bar near the Veteran's

Overleaf: The Doors on the pier at Venice Beach, 1967.

*The poetic side of Jim, revealed on stage with
Ray Manzarek.*

Hospital, where Jim got drunk and teased the wheelchair vets. He exposed himself and urinated in front of women in a public library. He climbed tall buildings on campus, drunk, and threw his clothes to the ground below.

And he dived deeply into film. Everywhere he carried ringed notebooks for scrawling his puzzling, startling and unusual ideas. The camera was an all-seeing god, he said; it satisfied a longing for omniscience. Cinema was the 'most totalitarian' of the arts, films themselves were 'collections of dead pictures which are given artificial insemination', and film spectators were 'quiet vampires'. There were two paths in the study of film (he wrote): one leading to spectacle, the other to a peep show. It came not from painting, literature, sculpture, or theatre, but from 'ancient popular wizardry . . . [from] an evolving history of shadows . . . a belief in magic', connected to priests and sorcery. The appeal of cinema, he wrote, lay in the fear of death, because it offered the 'illusion of timelessness . . . a kind of spurious eternity'.

Jim eventually published these notes himself (in 1969), as part of a slender book of 'poetry' called *The Lords: Notes on Vision*, and later they were republished by Simon & Schuster. They remain in print today after more than a dozen printings.

They were not only ideas, but also the wellspring for the student film he made. John Debella told me, 'I was the cameraman and star of Jim's film, although it's hard to say it had a structure coherent enough to have any single star. It was about a film-maker and a film-maker's eye. The camera and the eye saw all these horrible things. The things he photographed affected the photographer to the extent that his eyes became infected. The scenes I shot, him and I went to downtown L.A. and photographed in a lot of the sleazy bars and on Main Street [in Los Angeles' skid row]. Then we shot some stuff in his apartment, which included me and my girlfriend of the time, a big good-looking German girl. There was a shot of her dancing on the TV set in her underwear, with Nazis marching across the screen below. Another where she licks my eyeball, trying to cure the injury caused my eyes by the subjects of my photography. Then Jim took a hit off a joint, then we cut to the white line of the TV being turned off, fading to a single dot. It had a certain power to it, but I wouldn't consider it a good film.'

Terence McCartney Filgate was a professor who was, by his description, brought in from outside and given all the tough-nut cases for their final film. These were, he said, 'The people who caused trouble. Ex-cops, Mexican-Americans with chips on their shoulder, people like that. Jim was one of these. He was a very hostile guy. He had deep-set eyes and would stand around doing the Marlon Brando bit. The other students considered him uncontrollable.

'I was one of the few instructors who'd appear in student films. He was disorganized, seldom got anything together, never got a script out of him. I played a role in his film and part of it was as a man projecting the supposedly obscene movie. I was the projectionist. It was filmed in his apartment. He had *Playboy* centre spreads pinned up on the walls and had darts he'd thrown at them. He had a great hostility towards women. That's what struck me.

'There were far more colourful students than Jim. Felix Venable managed to kill himself with cirrhosis of the liver within three years or so and another one cut his girlfriend's heart out looking for the soul of his mother. Nonetheless, I remember Jim Morrison vividly. He was . . . different.

'Jim got a "D" for his film, by the way, because he never got it edited right. The splices came apart when he screened it. But he was not one of the poor students. The truth is, he was exceptional.'

Colin Young's comments are an echo: 'I didn't think Jim was the sort who could go the route in films. I didn't think he had the patience to hassle everyone long enough to get a film made. I felt he was an artist who hadn't got his act together yet. I considered his film interesting but unfinished. It was sort of irritating that he was obviously so talented, but hadn't really got it together.'

There was a third professor, Ed Brokaw. Colin Young told me that Brokaw was a permanent member of the staff and one of the best teachers, and he said it was likely that he got close to Jim. He said, 'He would've been drawn to any destructiveness, he would have smelt it and warmed his

The hostility perceived by some of Morrison's UCLA contemporaries was harnessed in his stage performances.

hands around that fire, because of how often that's connected with real talent.'

It was Spring and Summer 1965, a crucial time. Unknown to Jim, the previous fall, his father had sailed his carrier into the Tonkin Gulf, after North Vietnamese ships reportedly attacked U.S. destroyers. This resulted in the Tonkin Resolution, whereby Congress gave President Lyndon Johnson the power, in effect, to declare war. By Spring 1965, as Jim was completing his first semester at UCLA, the U.S. was bombing North Vietnam continuously.

As the war escalated so did the sound of rock as anthem after anthem for the sixties went roaring to the top of international record charts. In Los Angeles, a new band called the Byrds, conceived as a sort of American response to the Beatles, released 'Mr Tambourine Man'. While the Rolling Stones dominated the airwaves with '(I Can't Get No) Satisfaction', the Beatles shouted 'Help', a song that was followed in the Number One position by Bob Dylan's 'Like a Rolling Stone', which in turn was succeeded by Barry McGuire's 'Eve of Destruction'.

One of Jim's classmates was Ray Manczarek, (later, he would drop the 'c' from his name), a tall, lanky, bespectacled and somewhat older student from Chicago who played keyboards in a little band he had with his brother, called Rick and the Ravens. Jim didn't know Ray very well, but had respected him for refusing to cut out some nudity in his student film when the instructors requested it. One day Ray went up to Jim and said that because he was hired to deliver six musicians and only had five, would Jim like to join his band at a high school dance? Jim said yes and pretended to play a guitar and was paid $25 at the end of the evening. Afterward, Jim said it was the easiest money he'd ever made.

When Sam Kilman, a friend from Florida State, showed up soon afterwards, Jim suggested they start a rock band. Sam had played drums once upon a time, but he was incredulous at the suggestion. He asked Jim what the hell he was going to do. Jim said he was going to sing. Sam laughed and asked what they were going to call the band.

'The Doors,' Jim said. 'There's the known. And there's the unknown. And what separates the two is the door, and that's what I wanta be. Ahh wanna be th' dooooooorrrr . . . '

Of course nothing came of it.

(Incidentally, it was, of course, Aldous Huxley who said, 'There are things that are known etc,' first, but years later, Jim would get public credit for it because he used it in interviews and failed to credit the source.)

If Jim was only peripherally a part of the music scene in 1965, he was on the cutting edge of another revolution: the drug revolution. Probably no other place on the planet was more tuned in to turning on and dropping out in 1965 than Los Angeles. When Jim slipped away from UCLA, with his degree in theatre arts – and a diploma that had to be mailed to him, because, repeating his high school experience, he wasn't present when it was handed out – he started experimenting with anything that could be swallowed or inhaled.

'Jim was sitting there with some other friend and me,' Phil Oleno told me, 'and I had taken this belladonna and I still had the can. So I brought it out and I said, "Man, this stuff is a trip." I told him what it was. It was a foul-smelling green powder called Asthmador. It was made from belladonna, which is a poison, and they called it the Green Death. Asthmatics burned it in tiny quantities in a room to relieve them in attack situations. I knew about this shit from my father, the pharmacist. I told Jim how bad it was. I told him what it tasted like, how you talk to people for three days afterward that aren't there. He said, "You convinced me." And he started eating the shit. Just filling up capsules and swallowing them by the handful.

'Some people say, "Smoke Scotch broom . . . smoke bananas . . . get you high." Take something . . . anything. Even the worst shit. Drink a gallon of diesel grease and you'll get high. Some people will try anything. He would've. He'd have to find out. He'd have to take it and see. So he did. You know, the psychedelic adventure in those days was the great experiment. It was like a mountain you had to climb.'

III

THE POET

JIM HAD TOLD FRIENDS he was going to New York, but he went to Venice instead. Venice was a small beach community that was designed at the turn of the century as an upscale resort. It never succeeded, despite its complex of romantic canals, classical storefronts, and beachfront homes. Venice attracted a lot of attention in the 1950s as a magnet for Beat poets and jazz musicians.

In 1965, it was in a state of disrepair, a neighbourhood for the poor and for students and artists and senior citizens. Small cottages crumbled alongside stagnant waterways. People slept off their alcohol and drugs on a wide beach. Jim lived on the roof of an apartment building, rarely eating and losing 20 pounds in weight in a period of three months. He took LSD or smoked marijuana, or both, virtually on a daily basis, while scribbling poetry in a notebook.

These poems eventually became songs. In time, the body of work produced during this summer of narcotic dieting carried him, and the Doors, a long way. When he saw a black girl he liked, he described her as a 'dusky jewel' in a poem that began, 'Hello, I love you' (Three years later the poem was No. 1 on the hit parade.) 'Soul Kitchen' was written about Olivia's, a cheap restaurant on Ocean Avenue where plate lunches cost 85 cents. In 'The Celebration of the Lizard', he wrote about a little game, went crawling into his brain, to play the game called go insane.

Another of these poems was called 'Moonlight Drive' and it was this one that Jim recited one day when he encountered Ray Manzarek on the beach. Ray and his girlfriend Dorothy Fujikawa – who had been the nude in Ray's UCLA film – lived right on the beach. Ray was surprised to see

Jim, thinking he'd gone to New York.

The ensuing dialogue is well-known. Ray Manzarek is the source and I featured it prominently in *No One Here Gets Out Alive*. Oliver Stone recreated the scene in his movie, *The Doors*. It was perfect rock and roll myth, a Horatio Alger cliché

Jim said he had been writing poems and Ray asked him to sing one. When he'd finished Ray said those were the best rock and roll lyrics he'd ever heard and he suggested they start a band and make a million dollars. Jim said that was precisely what he had in mind, except the million dollars wasn't important. He wanted to go up like a Roman candle and make a bright light and then disappear.

Ray's band, Rick and the Ravens, was still intact, and the band actually released a 45 rpm record, but when it flopped, Ray's brothers said they were quitting. So Ray was glad to meet Jim. It gave him hope.

With assistance from a long-forgotten bassist, Jim and Ray recorded a demo disc that included 'Moonlight Drive', 'Hello, I Love You', a part of 'The Celebration of the Lizard', and another song whose title Ray can't recall. They began to take it around to the Hollywood record companies. Only a few bothered to listen, everyone said no.

Two new musicians joined the group, both members of a class in transcendental meditation that Ray was taking. John Densmore, a drummer, was the first. As soon as Ray met him, he asked him to come to a rehearsal and soon after that, John brought Robby Krieger, a guitarist. Both were from the West Los Angeles area, coming from upper middle-class lifestyles similar to Ray's and Jim's. John and Robby were well educated and had played together in a band called the Psychedelic Rangers. College boys who had discovered dope. They fitted perfectly. Or at least as close as anyone could fit with Jim.

And it worked musically. Jim was still shy and his voice was weak as well as untrained. But he seemed willing to try and his lyrics were compelling. Ray's keyboard influences were mostly in jazz and classical music, and he played it like a calliope. With Robby's spidery, blues-influenced bottleneck guitar and John Densmore's dramatic drumming, a three-way counterpoint was created where the musicians played against

*The Doors relax on Venice Beach, 1967. Jim first
discussed starting a band with Manzarek at
Venice in 1965 while he was living on a rooftop
near the beach.*

each other, creating a distinctive musical tension that suited Jim's dark, off-centre lyrics. By the time they started shopping the demo, Ray had discovered the Fender keyboard bass, and from that time forward he played the bass line with his left hand, the organ with his right.

Jim wrote one of his rare letters home. His brother Andy told me, 'He wrote a letter to dad about meeting some guys and they were starting a band. He said he'd tried to get a job after graduation and, majoring in cinema and all, he got nothing. He said he was sleeping on the roof of a building janitored by a friend. He said he was starting a group and "what do you think?" Dad wrote back and said he'd paid for college and Jim never did anything musically before in his life, never showed any musical ability, and "now you're telling me after I paid for four years of college you're starting a band! I think it's a crock!" Jim never took kindly to criticism and he never wrote again. Dad felt bad about it later, but he said at the time he felt he was right.'

After a bunch of crummy weekend jobs, playing for parties, they got the first important crummy all-week job, at the London Fog on the Sunset Strip. As noted earlier, they were paid poorly, and infrequently, and on the evening of their firing, a young woman named Ronnie Haran came into the place. She liked the band and, especially, she liked Jim. She was the talent scout for the Whisky a Go-Go and told her bosses, Elmer Valentine and Phil Tanzini, that the sexiest rock and roll star she'd ever seen was singing up the street and probably was available. Over the next four months, the Doors were the opening act at what was then the most important nightclub in Los Angeles. This did not mean the Doors were suddenly rich and famous, but rarely had a local band achieved as much so fast.

At approximately the same time, Jim and Ray found someone at Columbia Records who liked their 'demo.' Billy James was a former actor and a publicist for Columbia in New York – he was the one who broke the story about Bob Dylan's real

*Jim Morrison often maintained a deliberate image
of the 'loner'.*

name being Zimmerman - before moving to the West Coast, where he became an Artists & Repertoire (A&R) man, which meant he was mainly a talent scout. He signed the Doors to a six month contract and assigned a producer to record some songs. Before the contract lapsed or any recordings were made, they asked for and were given a release.

It was at the Whisky that Jac Holzman heard them. He was the somewhat stiff but erudite founder and president of Elektra Records, a company known mainly for its folk musicians. It was now 1966 and a year earlier, Bob Dylan had proved with 'Like a Rolling Stone' that it was possible to make the transition from acoustical to electric music without losing your audience or integrity. Jac figured he could do as much with his record company and recently had signed a Los Angeles band called Love. In fact, this was one of the bands that the Doors opened for and the band that Holzman went to see when he first was exposed to the Doors.

'We played for all the groups that came in,' John Densmore told me. 'The Byrds, Them, the Turtles, Captain Beefheart, and each time one of them came in, oh boy, we'd try to make friends with them, but we'd also want to blow them off the stage.'

Jac Holzman was not impressed. Ronnie Haran, who was helping Love with their career, told Jac that the Doors were good. When he visited the clubs, Jac always had a contract or two in his inside jacket pocket. When he saw the Doors the first time, he felt no inclination to reach for one.

In time, he changed his mind. 'I had seen Arthur Lee [leader of Love] and he had a very high opinion of the group and I had a very high opinion of Arthur Lee's opinion, and even though they didn't impress me, I kept going back. The third or fourth night out I heard a Baroque organ introduction to 'Light My Fire' which really impressed me. I made an offer to them that night, which was $2,500 per album, against a royalty of five per cent. At the time, they still hadn't extracted themselves from Columbia. So I went back to New York.'

It was June 1966. Jim was sleeping around, basically wherever night caught him, or with whomever he was with at the end of

the night. For about a month he lived with Ronnie Haran, who had been instrumental in getting the Doors into the Whisky. She said when she was trying to get the Doors hired, she had her girlfriends call the owners of the place and ask for 'that sexy motherfucker in the black pants'. She told me that Jim basically ignored her. She said one of her clearest memories of Jim, off-stage, was finding him day after day, sitting in her apartment smoking bag after bag of grass, one thumb-thick joint after the other.

Gay Blair was another woman in Jim's life at the time. Their relationship was more violent. 'He was one of the worst lays I ever had and I told him so,' she said. 'We had this knock-down, drag-out fight: lamp-throwing, fists and that. He'd gotten me down on the bed. I'd just bought a new outfit and he ripped it to shreds. Put his knees on my arms, legs on my legs and just spit all over my face. But then he turned so sweet. We went to Barney's after I'd taken a shower and he was so lovey-dovey.'

And then there was Pamela Zarubica, one of the all-time classic groupies of rock, better known in the rock milieu as Suzy Creamcheese. She showed up off and on for most of the rest of Jim's life. She was scrubbing floors at the Whisky while studying literature at Pepperdine University (she earned her degree in under three years) when she met Jim. 'If you're gonna rate somebody on a 1 to 10 scale, you're playing basketball, you're not making love,' Suzy said. 'What can you say about two teenagers, they get together and they don't really know that much about what's going on – because he didn't at that time – and neither did I – and it was wonderful, period. He was so fucking puritanical. He copped to it, too.'

Most important in Jim's life was Pamela Courson, the daughter of an Orange County high school principal whom he met during the summer on the Venice Beach. Pamela was nineteen, a fragile redhead with pale skin dusted with cinnamon freckles, enchanted by the hippie life and a little afraid of it. Jim took her under his wing, introduced her to psychedelic drugs and poetry. Although he was not faithful, it was to

Morrison as Adonis: women found him irresistible.

*Pamela Courson and Jim share a moment of
tenderness in Muir Woods, outside San
Francisco. Although their relationship was often
troubled, Pamela always remained Jim's sole
'cosmic mate'.*

Pamela he returned time after time, pledging his eternal love. They were, he said, cosmic mates.

'The first time I met Pam was when I went with Chris Stamp to a party that turned out to be an orgy,' Suzy said. 'Pam was stoned out on downers and talking shit in front of everyone, bad-rapping Jim: "You don't do that when you love somebody." The only other time I saw her was at the Whisky when Van Morrison was playing there and Pam came up and wanted to punch me out, but they pulled her away.'

Sometimes when the Doors weren't playing at the Whisky, Jim went to other bars on the Sunset Strip and 'sat in' with the house bands, usually singing 'Gloria' or some other contemporary rock standard. Pam frequently would go with Jim and for a short while she danced in one of the clubs, until Jim insisted she quit. By now, they were sharing a small apartment in Laurel Canyon. At the end of the evening, they walked home. Pam asked Jim to take a cab. He said no, the exercise was good for them. The truth was, he didn't have any money and had been drinking free at the bars in exchange for his singing there.

The soundtrack for Summer 1966 included Bob Dylan's 'Rainy Day Women #12 and #35' (in which Dylan sang 'Everybody must get stoned!'); the Rolling Stones' 'Paint It Black'; the Beatles' 'Paperback Writer'; the Mamas and Papas' 'Monday, Monday'; the Lovin' Spoonful's 'Did You Ever Have to Make Up Your Mind?' and Simon & Garfunkle's 'I Am a Rock'. It was the summer when the Beach Boys released 'Good Vibrations', reflecting the mood of the summer months, when everyone was feelin' groovy.

But it also was a summer remembered for its urban rioting; before it was over, there were disturbances in 28 cities in the U.S. The cry of Black Power rang out. And the U.S. bombed Hanoi.

It was also when Jim got bombed on LSD and delivered an inspired performance at the Whisky that got them fired. He failed to show up for the first set and when John and Ray went to fetch him, they found him crawling around on his hands and knees, mumbling something about 10,000 micrograms of acid. They took him back to the club and it was during the performance of 'The End' that the months-long employment at the club ended.

'The End' was a long, dramatic piece that was as much poetic recitation as it was musical composition. By now, the other Doors had learned to expect the unexpected from Jim, so they were ready to improvise around him, punctuating his poetry with appropriate mysterioso keyboard and guitar, and crackling drum exclamation points. This was the night that Jim introduced the oedipal verse, in which he pulled on his boots and walked on down the hall, checking first on his brother and sister; then walked on down the hall, entering a room where he confronted his parents.

'Father,' he whispered, 'I want to kill you. Mother? I want to . . . . . . FUCK YOU!'

The go-go girls in the glass booths in the club stood motionless. (As they frequently did, as the Doors were not easy to dance to.) The audience was mesmerized. And Phil Tanzini, one of the club owners, practically burst a blood vessel in his neck. On stage, the Doors finished the set – Ray Manzarek told me that they really didn't attach any importance to the new verse – and then filed upstairs to the dressing room, where Tanzini was waiting. He told them they were fired and would never work the Whisky again.

Once the Doors left Columbia, they signed with Elektra and made plans to record with Paul Rothchild, who had produced a number of folk albums for Holzman in the past and who had just been released from jail after serving eight months of a two-year sentence for possession of marijuana. Paul was not overly impressed by the band when he heard them at the Whisky, but he was happy to be on the street and working again and agreed to go into a studio.

The sessions went well, and were over in under two weeks. This was not unusual for first albums; after all, the band was playing material it had been playing for a period of many months. During the sessions, Paul's feelings about the band changed substantially. 'Every day we got something great,' Paul said. 'Jim was out of control on some days, but that was just another aspect of that phenomenon: the Jim Morrison spirit! Because we were recording when Jim was at one of his most insane points, when he was deep into acid.

'We tried many songs each day. That's one of the ways I record. The band does a few takes of one song, then moves along to another, so the song doesn't get stale. We tried 'The End' the first night and it didn't happen. One of the reasons it didn't happen was there were technical requirements that had Jim moving from inside a vocal booth to a mike in the studio, so the musicians could be cued properly, and Robby had to change guitars once during the song. There was choreography to think about. And Jim had to be in two different places while doing the song. He had to move. Because that's a live song on that album, performed from start to finish with no overdubs, thank you very much. We did 'The End' in essentially one take on the second night.'

Another night was equally memorable to Paul, but for destructive rather than productive reasons. Paul had returned home following the session, when he got a call from the girl who had left with Jim. She said Jim had jumped out of the car and was last seen headed on foot back toward the studio. When Paul arrived, he saw Jim, shirtless and without shoes, behind the locked studio gate.

'Where the fuck are your shoes?' he asked. Jim laughed and said he wanted to record. Paul finally argued him into climbing back over the fence and going home, where they listened to Donovan, the Rolling Stones, the Beatles, and Howlin' Wolf. Finally Paul went home.

As he entered his apartment, the telephone rang. It was the owner of the studio, who wanted to know what had happened. Sand from an ashtray had been thrown everywhere and a fire extinguisher had been emptied onto the mixing board and the instruments. Paul pleaded innocence. The owner said he found a pair of shoes in the studio; did Paul want him to find out who the shoes belonged to? Paul sighed and said no. The owner asked where he was supposed to send the bill for damages. Paul said, 'Elektra Records.'

IV

THE ROCK STAR

THE ALBUM was everything a first rock album should be: energetic and raw, marked by refreshing simplicity, yet polished by the confidence of familiarity. The boys had been playing these songs for months and all Paul had to do was capture them. Many reflected Jim's productivity on the Venice beach. The song he had written about a young black woman, '20th Century Fox', was there. So was his mysterious 'Crystal Ship' and the song about the restaurant in Venice, 'Soul Kitchen'. Bertold Brecht's 'Alabama Song (Whisky Bar)' and Willie Dixon's 'Back Door Man' gave the album roots sunk in cabaret and blues, respectively.

Of course, the song that capped them all was 'The End'. With its hypnotic and haunting lament of dread, its lyric ride on a strange blue bus, its image of a seven-mile-long snake, lost in a wilderness of pain (where children were insane), with its message of incest and patricide, it was a patchwork that came together to form what was one of the Door's longest and most depressing, yet seductive, songs. Whenever the Doors played the song, it stopped an audience dead. For this reason, the band usually played an up-tempo song right afterward, to return the audience to life. On the album, 'The End' was the final cut, leaving the listener at home to deal with his depression as best he or she could.

Recognizing the perversity of the Doors, and the possible commercial challenge that this represented, Elektra vowed to release a single that was non-threatening. The song selected was 'Break On Through', a rousing anthem celebrating risk, with a heavy message endorsing drugs. This lyric message worried Elektra, so one of the repeated refrains was edited, so that in the final version, Jim's cry that 'She get high/She get high/She get highhhhhh' was cut to 'She get/She get/She get.'

As disappointed as they were by the cut, the Doors did everything they could to promote the record. 'We called the radio stations,' John Densmore said. '"Hello, this is so-and-so from Torrance, will you play 'Break on Through'?" We did that over a hundred times a day. Robby did. Ray did. We all did. After a while, they told us to stop: "We know it's you . . . we know it's the same people." But we hyped it up to No. 11. We were scuffling.'

An image was forming, and the music was only a part of it. The rest of it was Jim. Right from the start, he seemed to have a clear image he wanted to create. When Elektra requested some basic biographical material for a press kit, Jim insisted his entire family was dead. And while he more or less went along with some of the other traditional questions - his favourite singers were identified as Frank Sinatra and Elvis Presley, his favourite colour was turquoise, his favourite food was meat – he could not resist when asked to give his philosophy.

'You could say it's an accident that I was ideally suited for the work I am doing,' Jim wrote. 'It's the feeling of a bow-string being pulled back for 22 years and suddenly being let go. I am primarily an American, second a Californian, third, a Los Angeles resident. I've always been attracted to ideas that were about revolt against authority. I like ideas about the breaking away or over-throwing of established order. I am interested in anything about revolt, disorder, chaos – especially activity that seems to have no meaning.'

He said, 'The world we suggest is of a new wild west. A sensuous evil world. Strange and haunting . . . '

For 1967, this was very heady stuff. This was, after all, when some of the biggest hit records included 'Snoopy vs. the Red Baron' by the Royal Guardsmen, The Turtles singing 'Happy Together', the Monkees' bouncy, up-beat 'I'm a Believer', The Young Rascals' 'Groovin'', and the Jefferson Airplane's Grace Slick celebrating 'Somebody to Love'. Surely with the lifestyle of the Haight-Ashbury district in San Francisco being recreated from coast to coast; gurus rising left, right and centre; and body paint and 'flower power' appearing in Johnny Carson's monologues, it seems a benevolent, if somewhat eccentric time. In stark contrast, Jim hinted that all was not sunshine and lollypops.

At the same time, their second single release was moving straight for the top of the record charts. 'Light My Fire', a lyric written by Robby Krieger, was a seven-minute track with a long instrumental break on the album. Cut to three minutes and released in June, it appeared at No. 7 on July 8th and was No. 1 three weeks later. From that moment forward, the Doors were one of America's premier rock bands.

Gloria Stavers was a pretty, thirty-something ex-model who edited *16 Magazine*, the most successful pulp monthly about rock for the pre-pubescent set. She fell in love with Jim.

She told me, 'He gave me a bracelet, called a vice, a ring-thing with a little slug of lead on it – it's what a sculptor uses to hold clay together in a kiln. It feels like stainless steel. Or a plumber uses it if he's fixing pipes together, he puts it around a joint. You twirl the heavy thing and it gets tighter and tighter and tighter. You could cut someone's circulation off if you wanted. He said he had found it in the gutter and it was so pretty he cleaned it up and gave it to me. Every time we saw each other, he checked to see if I was wearing it, so he would know I was his.

'I called him the Young Lion and he went along with that for *16*, but he'd say, "I'm not a lion, I'm a lizard, I am the Lizard King." Jim was David on the half-shell, Michelangelo's David, and the girl rising from the sea. He didn't comb his hair, he placed it with his hands. We almost had a fight once because I wanted to comb his hair. He screamed, "GET THAT COMB AWAY FROM ME!" I realized later he was right. It looked natural the way he did it. It was planned, yet natural.

'We had a photo session at my house. I told him to look at the camera and not at me and imagine the camera to be whatever or whoever he wanted it to be – a woman you want to seduce, a man you want to kill, a mother you want to upset, a boy you want to seduce; it could be a work of art, being admired, but it was always living, it was not a camera. And he

*Jim in leather jacket during the Gloria Stavers'
photo session.*

loved that! He responded to it like Marilyn Monroe did. He went through my wardrobe. He put on my coats, my jewelry. Finally he took the strand of beads and that's what he wore the next day for someone else's photo session – the single strand of beads and naked to the waist.'

As Gloria rushed her images into print, by summer, the Doors had a support group in place. Their agent, Todd Schiffman, was a middle-twenties guy from New York who wore checkered suits and wide ties and dedicated himself to doubling and then quadrupling the Doors' concert price, even before the record sales indicated they were worth the price. Mike Gershman, another New Yorker, whose background was in publicizing books, was hired by the General Motors of publicity, Rogers & Cowan, to head up their brand new pop music division; he was given the Doors as his first client. For managers the Doors had Asher Dann, a tanned Beverly Hills realtor who sold homes to the stars, and Sal Bonafede, who had some experience managing Dion and the Belmonts back in the 1950s and currently handled a mainstream singer named Lanie Kazan. Their lawyer was Max Fink, who had no experience in rock and roll at all, but who had come to the group through John Densmore's father; he would continue as Jim's attorney until long after Jim was dead.

In one way or another – either through lack of experience generally or in the specific field – they were novices, making it up as they went along. Max Fink was known as a criminal trial lawyer; books had been written about some of his cases. Mike Gershman learned about popular music by walking into a record store and saying, 'Give me an album by everyone with a strange name.' (Fortunately, he was exposed to some exceptional music, including recordings by the Byrds, the Beatles, the Grateful Dead, Jefferson Airplane, and the Mothers of Invention.) And as mentioned, one of their mangers was a realtor. If they were amateurs, however, they also were ambitious, undaunted by what could and couldn't be done.

With a Number 1 song, publicity comes easy, but the money comes more slowly. As the magazines lined up for interviews, and the performances increased in number, the group's collective lifestyle changed hardly at all. Jim was still sharing a small apartment with Pamela in Laurel Canyon. He still didn't have a car. The others also remained in small apartments, in Venice and West Los Angeles, and continued to drive the same cars they'd had for some time.

So it was the same, but it was also different. 'There was pressure,' John Densmore said. 'There were all these concerts and Jim had to get there on time, and he couldn't improvise the way he used to. We knew we'd have to have a new album. But it was all happening. You're on the road and everything's coming in.

'I think one of the main bad things about the whole scene is a group tries to make it, they work on their stuff for years or months or whatever, and get it really good, and when they get a hit, it's turned around. They find themselves practically writing in the studio. They can't play clubs. They can't let the songs evolve.'

John is right. Second albums seldom have the heat of the first ones. The material hasn't been seasoned. Things are done in a hurry. Despite this, the second Doors album contained many gems, in part because the group had not exhausted its repertoire on the first one. In fact, some of the songs had survived from the band's, and Jim's, earliest days. One of the oldest pieces was 'Horse Latitudes', the poem about horses jettisoned from ships caught in the doldrums that Jim wrote while in high school in Virginia. Others dated back to Venice, including the first song that Jim sang to Ray on the beach, 'Moonlight Drive'.

But it was another long, epic song-poem that once again dominated the album. This was 'The Music's Over', another mysterioso set-closer that the Doors had first played (in an unfinished form) at the Whisky. Listening to this eleven-minute musical opus made everyone think of the first album's lengthy song-poem, 'The End'. The images were different, but the patchwork lyric and by turns sombre and chilling mood were familiar. Now Jim said he wanted to cancel his subscription to the resurrection, and send his credentials to the house of detention. Before he sank into the 'big sleep', he wanted to hear the 'scream of the butterfly'. What had they done to the

'I am the Lizard King! I can do anything!'

earth? he demanded, echoing an environmental mood sweeping much of the counter culture.

'We want the world,' he cried, 'and we want it now!'

(Eric Van Lustbader, who would go on to write bestselling novels, was then a college student; he reviewed the album in a music fan magazine and said, 'Listening to *Strange Days* is like watching Fellini's *Satyricon*.')

The album's title – the LP was called *Strange Days* – and cover accentuated the perversity. The Doors, filling up the entire cover of the first album, were not present on the second. Instead there was an alley full of misfits, jugglers, clowns, and dwarves, with merely a Doors poster on a door behind them And the first single release from the album was the title song, 'Strange Days', the song that insisted that people were ugly when they're alone. Despite the immense popularity of 'Light My Fire', in this follow-up single, the fans stayed away in droves; the record didn't even make the chart, which was unusual for a follow-up single.

Elektra Records apparently decided to run back to the safety of a love song and next released 'Love Me Two Times'. Ahhhh, sighed the record-buying teenyboppers in his audience, that's more like it. 'Love Me Two Times' put the group back on the national charts.

At about the same time, the accountants at Elektra Records announced sales totals for the Doors for 1967, and did a little bragging. Said Elektra in a press release: 'The Doors now have the distinction of being the only group this year to strike gold with their first LP; furthermore, of all the groups making their recording debuts in 1967, only the Doors have had a million-selling single.'

This also was the year that Jim's father hit the top of his military 'chart', getting promoted to admiral; almost simultaneously, he discovered that his eldest son was a rock star. The Morrisons learned about Jim's new life when Andy came home with the first album. Andy told me, 'A friend of mine brought me the album and I'd been listening to 'Light My Fire' for months and didn't know. That's how we found out. We hadn't seen Jim or heard from him in two years. I played the album for my parents the day I got it, the day after my friend told me about it. Dad knows music. He plays piano and clarinet. Dad likes strong melody. He hates electric guitars. He likes the old ballads. He doesn't like rock. He listened to the album and afterward he didn't say a thing. Not a thing.'

There were two incidents involving the family after that. One I wrote about in *No One Here Gets Out Alive*, where Jim's mother tracks him down and shows up, with Andy by her side, at a concert in a hotel ballroom in Washington, D.C. All afternoon, she had pestered the other Doors and their road manager, Billy Siddons, trying to get to Jim, but Jim had given them strict instructions not to let her through. She found a seat in the front row and Jim finally acknowledged her when the band played 'The End' and Jim whispered, 'Father, I want to kill you,' then paused and looking directly into her face, he screamed, 'Mother . . . I want to . . . [the drums sounded a nervous tattoo] . . . I want to FUUUUUUUUUUUCCCCCK-KKKKK YOUUUUUUU!'

Jim never saw, or talked to, his mother again.

Andy told me about a visit he made to Jim in Los Angeles. 'I told him I enjoyed the concert in Washington,' Andy said. 'And I told him that mom felt really bad when he refused to see her. He told me if he called once, they'd expect calls every month or so. He said, "Either you break it or you're part of the family, there's no halfway point. Either you talk to them all the time, or not at all."'

Jim also gave his little brother advice. 'I talked to him about my being slow with the chicks, not getting any ass,' Andy said. 'I just finished high school. He said not to worry about it. He said he didn't get laid until he was at Junior College. He wanted me to feel like it was okay, like I was okay.'

In the months that followed their initial success, the Doors experienced typical stardom fallout. They decided Sal Bonafede and Asher Dann were ill-suited to manage them and they paid $50,000 to break their contract, borrowing the money from Elektra and replacing Bonafede and Dann with Billy Siddons, their middle-twenties, barefoot road manager.

Jim went out and bought a snakeskin suit. ('Where's the snake?' the receptionist at Elektra Records in New York asked the first time he showed up wearing it. Jim said the snake was 'inside.') The Doors stopped playing in small clubs and performed exclusively in larger halls.

And the media arrived at their door, dropping superlatives as frequently as Jim used to drop acid. Many of the reviewers were writing about the first album; due to the long delay between writing and publication, this was the way it was. Artists always have to experience their 'children' twice – first, when actually giving birth, and then again, when those creations are introduced to the public, usually as much as a year later.

Paul Williams, writing in *Crawdaddy*, one of the most confident and artistic of the monthly magazines, said the first album was 'as good as anything in rock . . . an album of magnitude,' and said the instrumental break in 'Light My Fire' was at least as good as sex.

Richard Goldstein wrote in the *Village Voice* that Jim 'pitches spastic love with a raging insolence you can't ignore'; Jim's lyrics, he said, were 'literate, concise, and terrifying'. Digby Diehl reported in *Newsweek* the great interview line about the Doors being 'erotic politicians' and said about Jim that once he got going, 'it's hard to say whose soul he's trying to save, his listeners' or his own.' *Vogue* said he wrote 'like Edgar Allen Poe blown back as a hippie'. And a columnist for the *Village Voice*, Howard Smith, said, 'There really hasn't been a major male sex symbol since James Dean died and Marlon Brando got a paunch. Dylan is more of a cerebral heart throb and the Beatles have always been too cute to be deeply sexy. Now along comes Jim Morrison of the Doors. If my antenna are right, he could be the biggest thing to grab the mass libido in a long time.'

By the time such accolades appeared in print, the Doors were promoting the second album and, soon after, were featured in *Life* magazine, attention they got not so much for their music, but for Jim's being arrested. This was the incident that cemented the band's position and role in the counter-culture, gave it a validity, a kind of reverse image of the *Good Housekeeping* Seal of Approval, which might have been called the *Rolling Stone* Stamp of Fuck You.

Publicity shot from Bobby Klein.

Jim slinked onto the New England stage, wearing black leather pants, a black shirt and a black jacket. About half-way through the set, he said, 'I want to tell you about something that happened just two minutes ago right here in New Haven. This is New Haven, isn't it? New Haven, Connecticut, United States of America?'

He talked about the evening so far. He said he had eaten dinner and had a few drinks and at the restaurant signed some autographs. He said he had talked about religion with the waitress. He said he met a girl in the dressing room: 'We wanted some privacy,' Jim told the audience. 'And so we went into this shower-room. We weren't doing anything, you know, just standing there and talking. And then this little man came in there, this little man, in a little blue suit . . . And a little blue cap. And he said, "What ya doing there?"

"Nothin'."

'But he didn't go away.'

Jim's words came out in slow motion, as the Doors filled in behind him in the fashion they always did when he improvised. Everybody punctuating the lines with guitar riffs, rim shots, and keyboard trills. Jim continued his story: 'He stood there. And then he reached around behind him . . . And he brought out this little black can of something . . . Looked like shaving cream. And then he . . . sprayed it in my eyes.'

That was when the New Haven police moved in, taking Jim and his leather pants off to jail, where they booked him for obscenity. A *Life* reporter happened to be in the audience with his daughter (a Doors fan) and a photographer who was present took some terrific pictures of Jim being arrested on stage. One of the pictures shows Jim confronting a cop on stage, holding the microphone to the officer's face.

'Go ahead,' Jim said, 'you got the mike. Say something.'

The cop remained silent.

It made great copy, and the reporter ended his story for *Life* with his little daughter wondering why the police got so upset.

With stardom came the TV shows. Jim's performance at *The Ed Sullivan Show* is well chronicled; I included it in my book and Oliver Stone featured it prominently in his film. Ed Sullivan and the show's director, who was Sullivan's son-in-law, visited the band in the dressing room and asked Jim to change one of the lines in 'Light My Fire'. When he sang 'Girl, you couldn't get much higher,' could Jim sing, 'Girl you couldn't get much better' instead? Jim said he thought he could do that and as he was leaving, Sullivan asked Jim and the others if they could smile.

Jim said, 'Uh, we're kind of a sullen group.'

The Ed Sullivan Show was broadcast live and Jim knew that, so when they got to the critical line, of course Jim sang, 'Girl, you couldn't get much <u>higher</u>!' With an emphasis on 'higher'.

Sullivan show executives said they had been considering a multiple-appearance contract for the Doors, but the group never appeared on the show again.

Jim really seemed to be enjoying himself. Over and over, he was presented with opportunities to stick it to the establishment, to tell authority to kiss his ass. In New Haven, nationally on *The Ed Sullivan Show*, and right in his mother's face. In this way, he came to embody the protest of his generation. All he needed now was something that linked him to the politics.

That came with a song called 'Unknown Soldier', included on the group's third album and released as a single in March 1968 as the follow-up to 'Love Me Two Times'. The single was not a commercial success, but the vehicle that the song provided made up for it. Although the era of MTV was many years away, in 1968, many bands were making films to promote their singles. Mainly this was done to satisfy the demand of all the music shows that had proliferated in the wake of successful television network shows like *Shindig* (ABC) and *Hullabaloo* (NBC). There must have been hundreds of such shows, at least one for each city in the U.S. There was no way for any band to appear on all of them, appearances which usually consisted of lip-synching to their most recent hit song, in exchange for which they also got to lip-synch to their new one. The answer: promise to appear 'live' when you were in the area and send a three-minute film to be used for now.

'Unknown Soldier' was the Door's first video and it served several purposes. Besides giving the band something they could send to all those television shows in Des Moines and Baton Rouge etc, Ray and Jim got to be film makers again. 'Unknown Soldier' was filmed, in part, on their beloved Venice Beach, where Jim was tied to a post and shot by a firing squad, spitting out a mouthful of blood in the film's closing frames.

On the stage, he re-enacted the same scene minus the blood. In concert, Jim was shot, collapsing to the stage, where he lay still, then finally began to twitch, only to rise like some re-incarnated hippie phoenix in leather pants to celebrate: 'The war is over! The war is over! It's all over! The war is over!'

Such theatrics put the Doors ahead of many of their contemporaries. This was, after all, a time when most bands just stood in a row of Nehru jackets and beads. Light shows were big during the period, with great molten lava-like blobs undulating on a movie screen behind the band. Strobe lights blinked the ballrooms into stop-frame frenzy and mirrored balls with spotlights shone on them – a holdover from when ballrooms really were ballrooms, in the 1930s – speckled the dance floor and dancers with hundreds of fleeting squares of light. When most bands played, the real show was on the dance floor, as hundreds or thousands of kids on acid and grass and who knows what else, maybe nothing at all, shook their new-grown long hair and moved their arms and legs in tie-dye, leather and lace. Waving sticks of burning incense. Tasting freedom.

While most bands just stood there, the Doors put on a show, in which Jim frequently seemed to be trying to exorcise demons, or conjure them up from some hidden and secret past. 'See, there's this theory about the nature of tragedy,' Jim said, 'that Aristotle didn't mean catharsis for the audience, but a purgation of emotions for the actors themselves. The audience is just a witness to the event taking place on stage.'

That quote came from an interview with Richard Goldstein for *New York Magazine* and is a good example of the personal performance that Jim continued to give. Interviewing Jim was also being a witness to an event. By now, Goldstein had established himself as a fan, an ally, while maintaining his reputation as one of the two or three most influential East Coast critics. Goldstein had praised the Doors in early performance in New York clubs (during the period when the first album was new in the stores) and on a subsequent visit to California, he met Jim beside a small lake near where Sunset Boulevard runs into the Pacific Coast Highway. Jim was in his element. He was smart and the interviewer was smart, so Jim gave the interviewer smart stuff. Like Aristotle, and more of his calculated, perfect quotes:

'The shaman, he was a man who would intoxicate himself. See, he was probably already an . . . uh . . . unusual individual. And, he would put himself into a trance by dancing, whirling around, drinking, taking drugs – however. Then he would go on a mental travel and . . . uh . . . describe his journey to the rest of the tribe.' A few minutes later, Jim said, 'I'm beginning to think it's easier to scare people than to make them laugh.'

In the article he later wrote, Goldstein responded with some of his own good lines, capturing Jim's mood: 'His voice drops an octave at the sight of a tape recorder, and the surrogate audience it represents. He gives a cautious, mischievous interview, contemplating each question as though it were a hangnail, and answering with just a trace of smile in the corners of his quotation marks. But he gets his scene across.'

A few days later, Goldstein followed the Doors into a recording studio where Jim, dressed in a new snakeskin jacket, and drunk, attempted to record a long poem called 'Celebration of the Lizard'. Jim retreated into the vocal booth with a bottle of brandy and began chanting 'Five to one/One in five/No one here/Gets out alive . . . ' The words echoed around the studio as the others stood by, waiting.

Eventually Jim emerged, sweat-drunk and announced, 'If I had an axe . . . man, I'd kill everybody . . . 'cept . . . uh . . . my friends.'

He said he wanted to buy a Mexican wedding shirt. Robby's girlfriend said, 'I don't know if they come in your size.' Jim said, 'I'm a medium . . . with a large neck.'

Overleaf: The Doors. L. to r: Manzarek, Morrison
Densmore, Tony Glover (on harmonica), Krieger.

Morrison's theatrics were ahead of his time.

'We'll have to get you measured, then.'

Jim replied, 'Un-uh . . . I don't like to be measured.'

'Oh, Jim, we're not gonna measure all of you, just your shoulders.'

Earlier in the evening, Jim cried, 'I am the Lizard King! I can do anything!' Apparently not. Paul Rothchild asked Jim to bring his notebooks to his house the next day to work on the lines, but for whatever reasons, the poem didn't work and it appeared on the album sleeve, next to a drawing of an iguana, but was never released on disc. On the Doors' third album, *Waiting for the Sun*, taken to market the following July, there would be no epic song/poem, breaking the pattern set in the first two.

It was about this time that I met Jim for the first time at Barney's Beanery, a plate lunch restaurant and late night bar about a block from the Doors' office. Jim was wearing a Mexican wedding shirt – medium, thick neck – and his leather pants. He had his publicist, Diane Gardiner, with him. I had dated Diane regularly a year or so earlier, had helped her get her first job out of college, working for a rock and roll publicist. I recently had signed on as the Los Angeles correspondent to *Rolling Stone*. The first story I had written for that publication was a review of a Doors concert. I said Jim's calculated falls into the audience were dramatic, but pretentious. If he ever saw the story, and remembered it, he didn't mention it during the course of the brief interview at Barney's. Later, Diane told me she had insisted that he be nice to me. Which he was. But he also gave me a zero interview. He was going through the motions, that's all.

He also was going through all the motions of a budding drunk at the time. When I left Barney's, Jim stayed, as he did during many of his afternoons. The days of drug experimentation were past. (He said that grass, once consumed by the kilo, now gave him the 'cosmic heebie-jeebies'.) By 1968, he had found his final drug of choice, a drug he had toyed with from high school onward, and the one that would define much of his life for what was left of it: alcohol.

Paul Rothchild spent as much 'creative' time with Jim during this period as anyone and he was, after the fact, anxious to put Jim's boozing into perspective. While he was willing to admit that Jim consumed alcohol to the same excess that he did his pharmacy, there was a difference.

'The great druggers who died as a result of their drugging were really great drunks, not great druggers,' Paul told me. 'That includes Joplin and Hendrix. As someone pointed out, they all had strong heads and weak bodies. Alcohol is the heaviest drug in terms of the damage it does. Jim, because he was an alcoholic, as opposed to being a great drugger, was lucid more of the time than he was out of it. A drugger is out of it most of the time. Ninety-five per cent of the time, Jim was together. And he spent the majority of his time by himself with a pen and paper and typewriter, mostly with a typewriter. He worked in notebooks enormously and he also typed out every single word of all his poems himself.'

However true that may have been – and Jim also continued to read voluminously – the stories of his drunken episodes were now too numerous for anyone to ignore. Frequently, they were violent.

In New York at a party thrown by Jac Holzman and Elektra Records, Jim smashed wine bottles and later in the evening, long after the party had ended, he paid an uninvited visit to Jac's apartment building, where he thundered on Jac's door and demanded entrance, while Jac remained silent inside.

Another time in New York, Jim crawled on stage at the Scene and wrapped his arms around Jimi Hendrix and tried to sing, eventually bringing the guitarist to his knees. A recording made at the time and later released as a bootleg album makes Jim sound like a steer being led to a slaughterhouse.

In Las Vegas with the author Bob Gover, who had met Jim while on assignment from *The New York Times Magazine*, Jim got drunk and picked a fight with a casino security guard and then called the arresting police 'ugly motherfuckers', escaping a threatened beating by the police only by minutes when Gover's friends bailed them out.

In the Hollywood Hills at a party at John Davidson's house, Jim and Janis Joplin got drunk together and Jim got so full of shit with Janis, she had to beat him off with an empty

Southern Comfort bottle. 'It was beautiful,' Paul Rothchild told me. 'Mr. and Mrs. Rock and Roll . . . '

Paul had a theory about Jim's drinking. He said, 'Medicine has recently discovered there's a certain kind of belligerent drunk, an overwhelming majority of whom are suffering from an enzyme deficiency and their bodies are able to absorb more than the usual one ounce of alcohol per hour. So they sit around a bar and as their friends get drunk, they don't, until all of a sudden they've consumed enough to become schizoid. They move from not drunk at all to very crazy drunk. With the right kind of pill, these people can drink like everybody else. But Jim didn't know about this. It wasn't discovered then. Jim must've had an improper enzyme balance. He was the classic example, the storybook case of this type of belligerent drunk. He stood in the middle of La Cienega Boulevard shrieking, "You're all a bunch of fucking niggers!" to the passing cars. He redesigned cars more than anybody I've known. He broke places up, all the time. One minute he was Bob Gover's best friend, the next minute he was pulling all of Gover's records out and throwing them all around the room and jumping up and down on them and destroying them.'

It got so bad that during the recording sessions for the third album, the other Doors took turns quitting or threatening to. Even Jim threatened to throw it all in, walking into the office once day, saying, 'I'm having a nervous breakdown and I want out.' Ray panicked and said, 'Six more months, just six more months!'

Finally, the other Doors decided to hire a 'baby sitter' and put Bob Dylan's old road manager, Bobby Neuwirth, on the payroll to glue himself to Jim and get him where he had to be, sober and on time. Neuwirth laughed when I asked him if he did it. 'I didn't,' he said. 'Jim wasn't the sort of guy you told him what to do. So I just hung out with him.' Robby Krieger told me that all Neuwirth did was learn how to do a hilarious Jim Morrison vocal impression, so they fired him.

Somehow, the album was finished and was a great success. Starting in September, *Waiting for the Sun* spent four weeks at the top of the American sales charts and following the medium success of 'Unknown Soldier', one of Jim's old poems that

survived from his post-UCLA days on the beach in Venice, 'Hello, I Love You (Won't You Tell Me Your Name?)', put the group back at the top of the singles lists. Other songs on the album included 'Love Street', written about the Laurel Canyon street (Rothdell Trail) where Jim had shared an apartment with Pam, and 'We Could Be So Good Together', another of his many songs about this erratic relationship. Compared to the previous two albums, it was a subdued effort that, except for 'Unknown Soldier', added little to Jim's image as some sort of mad, hippie shaman, but also did nothing to take away from it.

As the old cliché goes, it was the best of times and the worst of times. If 1967 ushered in a new era with the Summer of Love, 1968 shoved it back out the door again with the assassinations of Martin Luther King, Jr. (in April) and Robert Kennedy (in June), and the riots in the streets of Chicago that marked the Democratic Presidential Nominating Convention (in July).

Meanwhile Jim Morrison, probably the single most popular male vocalist in America, was spending most of his nights sleeping off too many drinks at the Alta Cienega, a cheap stucco, two-storey motel built around a tiny asphalt parking lot that was within staggering distance of the Doors office, Elektra Records, and most of Jim's favourite bars.

Babe Hill was a divorced ex-fireman and lifelong surfer, looking for something to do when he met Jim through mutual friends. Babe loved to party and he was strong enough to carry Jim to the motel at the end of the evening and loyal enough never to mention anything the following day. He told me that Jim rented an apartment at the Sunset Towers, a classic apartment building on the Sunset Strip where the mystery writer Raymond Chandler always had his heiresses live. When the building manager found out who Jim was, they wouldn't let him take occupancy.

'So we'd end up at the Alta Cienega,' said Babe. 'The place never filled up and whenever Jim wanted a room he'd get one.

Jim Morrison on stage at Winterland, San Francisco, December 1967.

Eddie gave him the worst room each time. Upstairs and hot, the television didn't work worth shit, and the air conditioning didn't do much. Ten dollars a night.'

More and more, Pamela was exerting her influence, or trying to. She hated the idea of Jim as rock star and urged him to quit the band to devote himself to his writing. Consequently, she had no time or courtesies to offer the other Doors and they, in turn, offered her the same friendship. She tried to get Jim to spend more of his nights with her in her apartment in West Hollywood. She fussed about the way he looked, pestered him about getting his clothes cleaned more frequently. She was jealous when he saw other women, even if they were groupies who followed him home to his motel room; in retaliation, Pam frequently went out with other men. Yet, it was to Jim that she was committed. In Venice when they met, Jim called her his 'cosmic mate' and that was the role she took for herself.

John Carpenter was a burly son of a longshoreman from San Francisco and a hard-drinking music writer for *The Los Angeles Free Press*, a weekly newspaper dedicated to the arts and unrest. He spent an entire day, from 11:30 in the morning until past midnight, with Jim and kept a tape rolling for much of the time. 'I recorded everything,' John said. 'The waiter where we had steak and eggs at the Hyatt. Babe coming up on a motorcycle. Right into the Phone Booth [a topless bar next to the Doors office], where Jim switched to Black Russians. He drank a lot of them. And I was trying to press him on political things, and during the middle of the interview he suddenly jumped up and over to where these topless dancers had been. Transcribing this interview was hell. The juke box was going and Jim was going "AWWWRRRRRR WAAAAAAARRRRRR ARRRRRGGGHHHH!" He stood up and started dancing with the topless dancers, and Babe went over and said, "Jim, let's go." And Jim stopped and we all went outside into the bright sunlight and went down to Barney's.'

As a courtesy, John said, he decided to let Jim see the interview before he published it and when he provided a transcript, Pamela took it. 'The interview showed Jim as a drunk,' said John. 'Which at the time wasn't what the Doors wanted

Jim to be. The Psychedelic Monster, okay, or the Lizard King, fine. Not the Drunk. So Pam blue-pencilled it and Jim wrote some things in the margins to include, which I did. But she blue-pencilled like crazy. She went through rambling thoughts of his which I thought showed him at his drunken best, and got the spirit of the interview over. She blue-pencilled it all the way through.'

There was also the Little Boy in Jim. John Carpenter hosted a half-hour, free-form programme for KRLA, one of the top rock radio stations in Los Angeles. After repeated invitations, Jim agreed to appear as an anonymous guest disc jockey on the show. John said, 'You remember what my show was like. It had no premise, and it was only a half hour anyway. So Diane Gardiner had dinner with Jim that day and he got very nervous and he kept leaving dinner and going into Diane's house to pick out records, saying , "Do you think John will like this?" It'd be Howlin' Wolf or some other blues singer.

'My show went on the air at 9:30 Sunday nights and it got to be 9:25, 9:28, no Jim. He was to bring records and be the host of the show, be the DJ. So he finally walked in, stone sober, and really scared, but the show was already over and I was getting ready to replay a show by Pink Floyd, which is what was scheduled to follow mine. Jim apologized profusely and I figured what the hell, so I started all over and he had stage fright. Which I understand in a way. Radio's different from coliseums, I suppose. And he came in and did yes and no answers to every question I asked, which made the half hour seem like ten hours. Finally I called him Jim and it was out who he was and he began to relax, but the show was almost over.

'Some of the records he picked were Howlin' Wolf, Muddy Waters, people like that, and you could tell he'd taken quite a deal of time picking them. He had this list of records he wanted to play and he had arrows on the list, things he wanted to talk about, pointing to this artist, that artist. After the show, we went over to the Tap Room, where the KRLA deejays go for drinks and that's when we should have recorded the

Overleaf: Jim on stage in Copenhagen, Denmark, 1968, during the Doors' brief European tour.

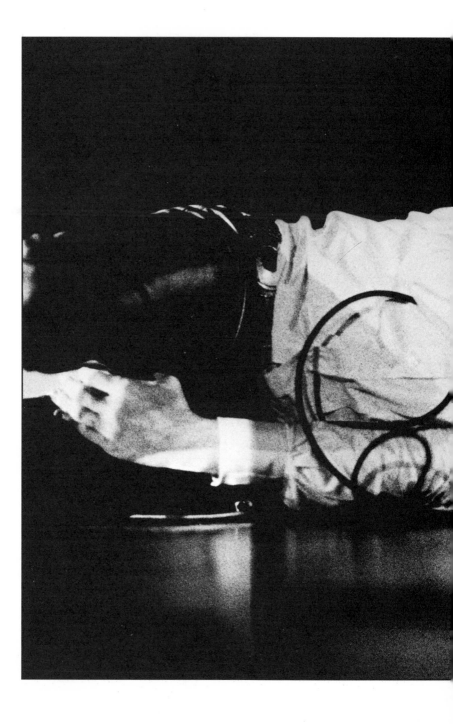

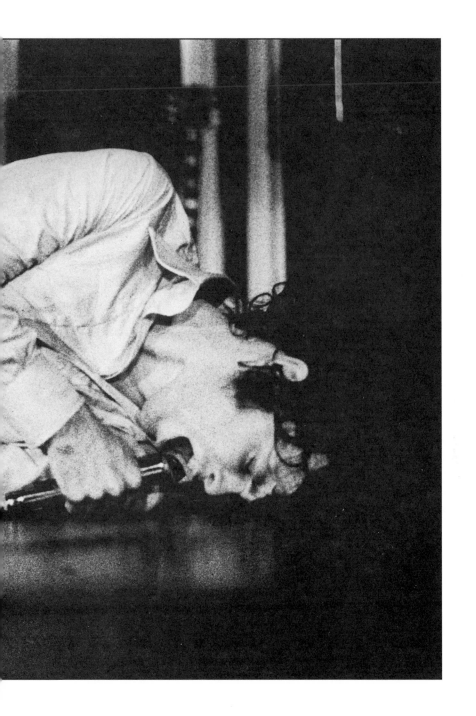

Morrison show. Jim got drunk and was just terrific. He was expounding on what was wrong with radio, what was wrong with the show we just did, and he was great. He was in his element, we were in a bar.'

Jim was pleased with the way the little film for 'The Unknown Soldier' had turned out and although the violence in that film had turned some people off – Bill Graham very reluctantly allowed it to be played in his Fillmore Auditorium when the band performed there, and many television stations refused to broadcast it – Jim urged the band to make more films. With Ray's interest in the medium rekindled, they assembled a small crew of amateur film maker friends and began recording some of the concerts. The plan was to cut the footage into usable promotional films for continued distribution to local television shows.

One of the two mainstays in the film crew was Paul Ferrara, who had known Jim from Venice and who had gone to high school with Babe Hill. He started as the Doors' still photographer and produced a souvenir book that was sold at concerts. He was regarded as the Doors' resident 'flower child'. The second was Frank Lisciandro, another film school graduate who with his wife Kathy, a nurse, served for two years in Togo, West Africa, in the Peace Corps before returning to Los Angeles. A few months after Frank joined Paul, and set up an editing room on the ground floor of the small, two-level Doors office building, Kathy went to work as the band's secretary-receptionist. Frank was the band's zen expert, very serious, dedicated to getting everything right.

For ten months they filmed the band, not just in concert, but backstage. The idea now was to make a full-length documentary. A piece of paper went up on the office bulletin board, soliciting suggested titles. Most came from Jim's lyrics. One of John Densmore's choices was a favourite: 'Mute Nostril Agony' (from 'Horse Latitudes'), but the final choice was 'Feast of Friends' (from 'The End').

Billy Siddons continued as their manager, rarely offering any guidance, but capably handling the day-to-day headaches that inevitably accompanied association with a rock band.

Jim samples some of the local wine in Frankfurt,
Germany, September 1968.

'Bill never knew what trip Jim was on,' Frank Lisciandro said. 'He wanted to be the entrepreneur/manager/concert producer, but Robby and Ray and John never really gave him that trust and Jim didn't give a shit about any of it. Occasionally he would, but for the most part he'd rather just hang back and not do anything, hoping Bill wouldn't round up any gigs, so he wouldn't have to go out on the road. Bill had it rough. He was nineteen or twenty when he started.'

Vince Treanor was the band's equipment manager. He was an eccentric, so intelligent that he filled in for his science teachers in high school when they were sick; later he got into stock car racing and designing pipe organs. He first saw the Doors at the New Haven concert when Jim was arrested, went to work soon afterward and quickly picked up a reputation as someone who could tear a broken amplifier apart and put it

back together again almost instantly, in the middle of a concert, in the dark. He admitted to trying to take over the Doors soon after Billy was named manager. Rather than fire him, Billy gave him a raise and elevated him to road manager. It was that kind of group.

Diane Gardiner was still the publicist, booking the interviews and seeing that Jim arrived on time. Jim insisted that all business meetings to discuss those interviews be held at the Phone Booth, the topless bar next to the Doors office. The public relations firm that Diane worked for also represented the songwriter Tim Hardin and one day Diane took Tim to the Doors office with her. The three of them went next door.

'Jim was interested in topless dancers and how they felt,' Diane said. 'He had a real empathy for them. He would go to those places and he would sit there and he would applaud. He'd be a great audience. Anyway, we were sitting there, Timmy and Jim and I, and "If I Were a Carpenter", one of Timmy's songs, came on the juke box, by the Four Tops. It was Tim's moment of glory. And Jim was saying, "See, man, you never can tell what can happen – your song's being played at the Phone Booth with a topless dancer shaking to it." Afterward, Jim called the dancer over, he knew her, and he introduced her to Timmy, and Timmy shook hands with her. It was one of those really rare moments in rock and roll.'

The Doors' success was not exclusively American. For a decade now, rock and roll had been an international 'language' and so Jim and the boys went on the inevitable European tour. The last concert before leaving was at the Singer Bowl, on Long Island, a concert ultimately included in *Feast of Friends*. Jim is shown exiting a long, black limousine and walking toward the stage. The soundtrack is a single word, repeated by the crowd: 'Morrison . . . Morrison . . . Morrison . . . ' After the concert, Jim is shown sitting backstage with some of the fans, who are bleeding from the riot that ended it. The Lizard King at rest, sympathetic.

Jim Morrison in New Haven, Connecticut. His all-leather outfit set a universal rock style.

And then it was off to London, where the group participated in a black-and-white documentary for Granada TV and performed with the Jefferson Airplane at the Roundhouse, a nineteenth century circular brick building that had originally been a railway engine shed with a turn-table, but which in 1968 was the primary rock music venue in London. The only thing remarkable about the show, which was one of the Doors' best, was that it was preceded by an argument over which band would close the show, the preferred position. Billy Siddons took the position that if the Doors went on first, the audience would be so exhausted, the Airplane would never get them back up again. The Doors went on last.

It was in Amsterdam where it fell apart. The two bands were still sharing the stage and Jim had consumed a lump of hashish and more alcohol than anyone knew. When Vince Treanor arrived backstage he saw Jim sitting at a piano, 'gripping the lip area of the Steinway with his left hand, struggling to stay semi-erect'. Vince recalled, 'We told the Airplane to extend their set, keep stalling. Then we told the stage crew to take time in changing the set-ups, make it the slowest change between bands in history: stall, stall, stall. We told the Airplane staff to move slowly. They'd move stuff off, we'd move it back, playing the shell game with the amps, keeping the audience watching and occupied at least a little. Finally, we made an announcement that Jim couldn't perform because of fatigue and illness, and if the audience was willing, performance by the three other Doors would go on, or they could get their money back. The audience applauded the first idea and the Doors did both sets without Jim.'

Jim was taken to the hospital and the next day and on the basis of what Jim said – that he was just tired from performing – the doctor surmised that Billy Siddons was working his talent too hard. The doctor told Jim to tell Billy it would be a good idea to schedule fewer performances and when he reported this to Billy, Jim grinned widely

Jim Morrison on stage at the Roundhouse,
London, where they played a set with the Jefferson
Airplane in 1968.

mischievously. Billy, of course, was furious.

When the rest of the Doors and crew returned to the U.S., Jim rejoined Pam in London, where she had leased a large apartment in the exclusive Mayfair district. There, they were met by Michael McClure, one of the 'Beat Generation' poets whom Jim so admired when he was in high school in California. Michael had written a play about Marilyn Monroe and Billy the Kid (*The Beard*), and a Hollywood producer thought Jim should be cast as Billy. The first night the two got together, they got very drunk and three times attempted to hire a taxi to take them on what would have been an all-night ride to England's Lake District, to see Wordsworth's home. But the neighbourhood bobby, drawn to the address by all the noise, insisted they stay at home.

'We'd talked about poetry the night before and when I came downstairs the next morning I found a large stack of poems,' Michael said. 'I knew Jim was a poet and I enjoyed his singing, but I never had seen any of his poetry. I sat down and read the stuff and I was terrifically impressed. These were the poems that appeared in *The New Creatures*. Later Jim told me they had been sorted out by Pam, who'd edited it down from a much larger manuscript at Jim's request. She didn't like four-letter words in his poetry and what he left in, Pamela took out. He seemed to explicitly rely on Pamela.

'I think about the poem about Ensenada. It reminded me of William Carlos Williams' 'The Red Wheelbarrow,' one of the great objectivist poems. Jim and I talked a lot about putting his poem on a billboard on Sunset Boulevard. With no signature. Just the poem.'

Jim also discussed self-publishing with Michael, who had done that once. Michael urged him to do it. There was no shame or immodesty attached, he said. Many of the best writers in history had paid to have their work published. Jim starting making plans to do just that, but he also wanted a larger audience. So when he returned to Los Angeles, he took a box of poems to Michael McClure's agent, Michael Hamilburg (who was also a friend of Pam's sister Judy). Jim explained his

Raw and untrained – Jim on the move.

concerns about the poems selling on the basis of his being a rock star. If they found a publisher, he said, when the book appeared, he did not want his picture on the cover and he wanted it to be 'By James Douglas Morrison'. And, he said, the book would be dedicated to Pamela.

This did not mean that Jim was faithful. Now, as before, Jim shared the beds of other women, and welcomed strangers into his motel room. Jim liked to walk the streets of West Hollywood and frequently when he met a young woman, no matter how overweight or unattractive, he took her back to the tiny room. 'Jim was one of the last great mercy fucks,' one of his close friends said. 'I think that every woman in Los Angeles had slept with him,' said Tina Robbins, an artist and designer he had met in California but subsequently moved to Manhattan. 'I certainly wasn't naive in that regard. We had our own brief affair for a week or so in New York. He was very nice to me, but erratic – he had a sadistic streak that if allowed to come out, would. He did his best to hurt my feelings later when we ran into an acquaintance of his and he pretended he didn't know my name. It made me furious.

'I had a friend, whom he also slept with. He called her up one day and asked her to come over. When she got there, the house was dark, and she stumbled around. When her eyes had adjusted to the gloom, she saw him in bed with another woman. That was his sadism coming out; he'd done that just to hurt her.'

At this time, Jim also began a relationship with another woman in New York who, later, assumed a more important role in his life. This was Patricia Kennealy, the quirky, intelligent editor of *Jazz & Pop* magazine. They met in Jim's suite at the St Moritz Hotel when the Doors performed at Madison Square Garden. Rock groups just did not perform in this hallowed hall in 1969, so the booking attracted a lot of media attention. When she walked into the hotel room, Jim stood up and politely shook her hand and she thought, 'Dear, God, his mother taught him manners when he was a kid and he remembered them.'

Diane Gardiner, who had invited the press to the hotel the day after the concert – which had gone well – remembered it

In one of his many run-ins with the law, Jim is arrested on stage by a policeman at New Haven, Connecticut.

as a 'real strange day. All the press arrived and there was Jim, talking to everybody and he was being wonderfully funny. But then he got progressively drunk and was falling flat on his face. I was getting nervous and upset and my sense of humour was wearing thin. He got drunker and I tried to get the press to leave. They couldn't believe how anybody could drink that much and, second, they were mesmerized by how charming he was.

'Finally I said, "Well, Jim, come on into the other room. We gotta call this man with whom you have an appointment." And he went with me, and I said, "Look, Jim, you're a great guy for meeting the press and all, but now you're . . . doggone it, you're falling down . . . and I just got this job to do, I could lose my job, so I'll go out and tell them you had to go meet this man."

'By now, Jim had fallen across the bed and he just looked up at me and he said, "I want to fuck you." At that time, I took it as a real insult, although there was that old part of me going, "Gee whiz, I'd like to fuck you, too." So I just said, "Sure Jim, sure, Jim." Later I found out he didn't like women who weren't feminine. He doesn't like it when women get kind of brash. He thought I was being too mechanized, I found out later. Anyway, we didn't fuck and the press people didn't go home and Jim didn't meet this person I'd made up and he went back out into the front room.'

This is when it turned strange. One of those present was Ellen Sander, a young, attractive brunette who wrote for the *Saturday Review*. She once had called Jim a 'Mickey Mouse de Sade' and Jim hadn't forgotten it. He urged her to sing a song for the room full of people. She said she didn't sing, she was an audience. He insisted. She declined again, almost on the verge of tears. Finally Jim screamed at her, 'Sing, goddamn it! Sing!' In a small, pitiful voice, Ellen sang the first lines of the Beatles song 'Hey Jude'.

Everyone in the room was stunned. David Anderle, a young artist who ran the Elektra Records office in Los Angeles, had brought along the even younger composer-in-residence for the New York Philharmonic Orchestra, Fred Myrow. He, like Patricia Kennealy, didn't get to know Jim well this day, but would. Others from the New York press were present as well and they were appalled by what Jim had done to Ellen. Out of respect to Ellen, no one wrote about the incident, but Jim's reputation as Mr. Charm plummeted.

Patricia Kennealy and Fred Myrow viewed it more charitably. Patricia told me that when they shook hands, 'there were sparks, from the friction on the carpet'. She also admits to a different kind of spark that she felt in her heart, although it would be more than six months before they began their relationship. Fred Myrow, on the other hand, found in Jim a kindred soul with whom he identified immediately.

'When we met,' Fred said, 'he gave me the heaviest first line I've ever had: "Fred, if I don't find some way to develop within a year, all I'll be good for is nostalgia."' Fred had gone to the Philharmonic on a commission from the Dmitri Metropolis Foundation to write an evening of music that Leonard Bernstein would premier, based on an African primitive funeral ritual. While he had found this intellectually stimulating at the time, and now it was of interest to Jim Morrison, in time Fred came to question it. While doing a subsequent concert in Berlin, he heard the first Beatles album and began to think that what he was doing was 'out of joint with the outside world. There was a life and vitality in the Beatles' music which was not in my main line of work, which was giving concerts of avant-garde contemporary music. For two years I sat in the Carnegie Recital Hall and when I met Jim, I knew we <u>both</u> had to make a move. It cemented our relationship immediately.'

Back in Los Angeles, Jim turned his attention to the dramatic stage when the Living Theatre came to town for a week of performances at the University of Southern California. Jim had known of the revolutionary, communal theatrical troupe for some time, pumping the *Free Press* writer John Carpenter for details when he said he had a friend in the group; reading avidly an article about the actors and their founders, Julian Beck and Judith Malina, in *Ramparts* magazine; and finally from Michael McClure, who had known the Becks in New York ten years earlier. He asked the Doors' secretary to buy 16 front row tickets for each of the five performances.

Paradise Now was one of the troupe's most controversial performances and the one they decided to put on in Los Angeles. 'It's a play in which at the end of eight different sections, we play at each section an encounter with the audience,' Judith told me. 'We bring up a category of subjects. We're all on the stage together, rapping, having all kinds of encounters and relationships. Sometimes I'll be with two people in a relationship in one scene and Julian will be somewhere else in the theatre in another scene. The tone is very aggressive. Sometimes that aggression is very positive. Sometimes it isn't. But our intention is to turn it into something very positive, take it to paradise by bringing out all the hostilities.'

Julian added, 'The play also traces different revolutionary steps. The effort is to go from one step . . . one run, to another . . . and keep carrying the public along. We challenge the public to play different roles.'

The roles came out of rules, they said – like not being able to travel from one country to another without a passport, and not being able to live without money, and not being able to smoke marijuana, and not being able to embrace nudity. As indicated by the Becks, the play changed substantially from performance to performance, but the structure remained, along with some of the more powerful scenes. Each night at the end of the performance, different cast members cried out:

'I'm not allowed to take my clothes off!'

'The body itself of which we are made is taboo!'

'We are ashamed of what is most beautiful, we are afraid of what is most beautiful!'

'We may not act naturally toward one another!'

'The culture represses love!'

'I am not allowed to take my clothes off!'

It was at this point that the actors stripped down to their underwear, making the point that they had reached society's limit. They then cried, 'I'm not allowed to take my clothes off! I am outside the Gates of Paradise!'

That was when the Los Angeles Police Department moved in and stopped the performance. Jim was sitting in the front row. The next day the Doors were scheduled to appear in Miami.

V

THE DRUNK

JIM WAS DRUNK when he arrived at Miami's Dinner Key Auditorium.

He was late and the Doors and the audience, which was crushed into a large open space without chairs, were restless. The Doors had agreed to accept $25,000 for the show, instead of the usual 60% of the gross, when they were assured that the gross wouldn't exceed $42,000. Then the seats were taken out by the producers, allowing them to sell an extra 7,000 tickets, and when the Doors discovered the awful conditions in the auditorium, they were outraged. So when Jim finally arrived, the tension between the producers and the Doors was substantial while the conditions on the auditorium floor were worsening. All those bodies packed into a space too small began to generate a collective heat that blended with the assorted drugs thousands in the audience had ingested or smoked before entering.

The tape I have of the concert reveals two things: (1) Jim was entirely too drunk to perform, and (2) the 'performance' he gave more or less followed the outline of the Living Theatre's play, *Paradise Now*, almost as if it were scripted. Over the next hour, the Doors repeatedly tried to get Jim on track musically, starting and abandoning several songs when Jim was unwilling, or unable, to sing. While Jim interacted with the audience, sharing drinks with the ones closest to the stage, then standing up and bellowing, 'I'm not talking about a revolution! I'm talking about having a good time!'

Within ten minutes Jim turned the plea for a good time into an awful time. It started when he told the audience, 'I'm lonely. I need some love, you all. Come on. I need some good times. I want some love-ah, love-ah. Ain't nobody gonna come up here and love me, huh? Ain't nobody gonna love my ass? Come on!'

And that quickly degenerated into Jim calling the audience 'a bunch of fuckin' idiots'. What happened after that is debatable. In *No One Here Gets Out Alive*, I took the position that Jim did not expose himself, as he was later charged by Miami police. Vince Treanor, the band's road manager, was on the stage behind Jim and he said that when Jim unzipped his leather pants, he was wearing bulky boxer shorts underneath them – unusual for Jim, because he rarely wore underwear. Vince said it was Jim's intention to go only so far, just as the Living Theatre had done, then stop. Besides that, Vince said, he crouched behind Jim put a hand against Jim's back and pulled back on his belt, making it impossible for Jim to lower his pants.

There were others who testified differently. They said Jim definitely exposed himself. Not long ago, I heard from a young woman who said she was present at the concert and in a four-page letter she insisted that it was true; she remembered Jim's penis, after all these years, vividly.

The weird thing is that none of the charges against Jim were filed for several days. In fact, during the performance, Jim had removed a police officer's hat and sailed it into the audience like a Frisbee. Backstage, the officer laughed and appeared to enjoy meeting the band, as Billy Siddons gave him a couple of hundred dollars for the hat.

Jim was vacationing in the Caribbean when, on March 5th, 1969, the Dade County Sheriff's office issued a warrant for his arrest, charging him with lewd and lascivious behaviour (a felony), indecent exposure, open profanity, and drunkenness (all misdemeanours). A day later he added another charge, simulated oral copulation on his guitar player, Robby Krieger. At some point during the evening, when Robby was performing a solo, Jim had dropped to his knees in front of him, someone had taken a picture, and that was regarded as evidence that Jim was mimicking a sexual act.

At first the Doors thought it was a joke and even when they realized it wasn't, it was a while before they took it seriously. After all, this wasn't the first time. No one had forgotten New

Haven. As Ray recalled, 'There wasn't anything he did in Miami he hadn't done a lot of other times.'

Besides, drama was a part of this game, an integral part of every Doors act, on and off the stage. The destroyed recording studio in 1967 and the damaged hotel rooms since. The scenes with the swarming groupies. The soaring roar of love that greeted the Doors in concert. The hundreds of thousands of dollars that came washing in. Jim's mythic drunks. It was all so larger than life. What the hell difference did another drunken performance in another city mean?

As it turned out, it meant virtually everything. By the end of March, the FBI entered the case, charging Jim with unlawful flight from the country (to the Caribbean for his vacation following the Miami concert). It was a made-up charge, like the one saying he was trying to have oral sex with Robby.

At the same time, a 'decency' movement blossomed in Miami, evolving into a show at the Orange Bowl starring Anita Bryant and Jackie Gleason, assailing the Doors and everything their lead singer allegedly personified. The movement received national attention and the media started running long stories about the foul-mouthed, pants-dropping Jim Morrison. Not only the media, but the trade press as well, including *Boxoffice*, a monthly newsletter that went out to all the concert hall managers in the country. According to Billy Siddons, in the next month the Doors lost a million dollars in bookings.

'The word was out,' Ray Manzarek told me. 'Get the Doors.'

For Jim, it was a blessing in disguise. While he hated the injustice as much as the others, the cancelled concerts gave him precious time to work on his other projects and in the months that followed, he privately published two collections of his early poetry. He called his books *The Lords* and *The New Creatures*.

The first was no more than tastefully reproduced and packaged pages from his leftover UCLA notebooks, recording his eyeball-slashing thoughts about film. It was produced on 82 sheets of expensive paper stock and unbound, contained in a royal blue box that you folded around the poems and tied with a ribbon. The second book measured only four inches by

five and was bound in a simple brown cover reminiscent of school workbooks. The titles were embossed in gold and the author was identified as 'James Douglas Morrison'. He had 100 copies of each printed and for a long time, most of them were stacked against a wall in the Doors office. Nonetheless, Jim was thrilled.

During the same period, Jim also changed his image and agreed to do two key interviews. One was with me, for *Rolling Stone*. After Miami, *Rolling Stone* had depicted Jim as a buffoon and I knew he was more, or less, than that. At that time, *Rolling Stone* ran something called 'The Rolling Stone Interview' – inspired by the *Playboy* interviews, which appeared in question-and-answer form. Jim had never been interviewed by *Rolling Stone* in that fashion. I suggested to the editor, Jann Wenner, that we 'do' Jim. He agreed and after some consideration, Jim also agreed, and we got together over a tape recorder off and on for two weeks, over lunch, and over lots of beer.

The interview appears elsewhere in this book, so I won't go into it now, except to say that Jim remained intelligent and articulate from start to finish and he never got out of line. He got drunk, but never outrageous, or violent. I don't know if this was intentional, or lucky. I suspect it was intentional. Now that he had *Rolling Stone*'s attention, he was determined to charm, to rectify, and clarify.

After one of the interview sessions, conducted in the Doors' office, Jim suggested we go next door to the Phone Booth for a drink. As soon as we entered the club, 'Love Me Two Times' dropped onto the turntable and one of the topless dancers began to shake her two times for Jim. After the dance, Jim called her over and shyly introduced me as his friend. I confess being much more impressed by the dancer's thoracic development than by Jim's hyperbolic friendliness.

The last interview session ended in a recording studio, where Jim read the text of his latest poem, 'American Prayer' (which also would be privately published some months later). He asked that the poem run in *Rolling Stone* next to the inter-

A moment of contemplation: Minneapolis, 1968.

view and suggested that perhaps the Doors would be interested in promoting their next album by letting me interview them and releasing excerpts as radio spots. I admit I was flattered, although I didn't think it was a serious suggestion. Which it wasn't. And the poem was published with the interview, copyright by James Douglas Morrison.

Jim wanted to be taken seriously. Getting some of his ideas across, and appearing to be rational and intelligent in *Rolling Stone* represented a large step in that direction. *Rolling Stone* wasn't even two years old, but it was regarded as the hippest publication of the sixties, an arbiter of the culture, and its approval could be equated to the *Good Housekeeping* seal.

I came away from the interview liking Jim. He was playful. He had a sense of humour about himself. We were talking one day and he smiled and said, 'This is really a strange way to make a living isn't it?' I believe he meant it.

The other important interview he gave was for Channel 13, WNET in New York. Nowadays we call this kind of television PBS. Then we called it 'Educational Television'. And that's why Jim was there, to meet the hip New York press and to 'educate' them and the hip New York audience.

The show, *Critique*, opened with the Doors performing their newest single release,'Tell All the People', a song of Robby Krieger's that Jim disagreed with so much that for the first time he insisted that individual writing credits appear on the recording. (Royalties remained evenly shared, as always.) He said it made him sound like he wanted people to follow him. Jim had decided early in life not to trust leaders and a leader is the last thing he wanted to be.

There followed a collection of songs that spanned most of the Doors' career, and this, in turn, was succeeded by a pyrotechnical, adjective-to-the-floor statement by Richard Goldstein, who had been one of the Doors' most avid champions in the *Village Voice* and other publications in the early days. He said the Doors had become so popular, they were 'able to leap tall groupies in a single bound' and then quoted Jim, saying, 'When you make your peace with authority, you become an authority.' Richie then introduced excerpts from an interview he did with the Doors a week earlier. In this, he referred to a story he wrote called 'The Shaman as Superstar'. He asked Jim if he thought rock heroes could perform a 'religious function for kids, for young people'.

Jim said he had read about the shaman and thought the shaman emerged because the people of his tribe pushed him into it. Richie said he thought a shaman was needed in a time of social turmoil, an obvious reference to the huge political and social battle being waged over Vietnam, sex, drugs, rock and roll, and a hundred other things at the time.

Jim said, 'I don't think the shaman, from what I've read, is really too interested in defining his role in society, he's just more interested in pursuing his own fantasies.'

The words came like beads on a string: well-formed, and orderly. It appeared clear that Jim was thinking. Surely, not everyone was able to follow him, but he was interesting.

His visual image was worth noting, too. Gone were the leather pants, replaced by baggy striped jeans. Always lean, now he had a obvious paunch, the dubious trophy that booze awards. That strong jaw and those beautiful sunken cheeks now resided behind a full beard. With his thin cigar and sunglasses, Jim now looked like a hip, fat Che Guevara. Gone was the rock hero that Richie wanted to talk about.

The show closed with Jim's performance of 'The Soft Parade', a long song-poem that was named for Jim's description of people walking along Sunset Boulevard, giving the Doors' new album its title. This album, recorded the previous winter, and released in July 1969, was not one of the group's best. The Doors themselves came to regard the album as the one they did with 'the La Cienega Symphony', named for the avenue that passed the Elektra studios and for the many classical musicians hired to provide backup on several of the songs, most notably on 'Touch Me', another Robby Krieger song that went to Number 1. (Ironically, Robby had called the song 'Hit Me', a bitter response to a faltering relationship with a woman, and it was Jim who suggested changing 'hit' to 'touch'.)

The Doors were not the only band to incorporate classical back-up during this period. But they probably were the least suited to it. The distinctive Doors sound was noted for its compelling coarseness and for its theatrical silences. With strings added, there were no silences and the gritty blues were diluted, and the Doors crossed over from rock to pop. In a word, they were overproduced. However, the album sold well. The Doors were an established commercial success, Miami or no Miami – perhaps, in part, because of Miami.

Actually, Miami was becoming a very big deal. When the Doors finally started to get work again, there was something new in the contracts. A special rider specified that if Jim was obscene, or profane, the Doors would be liable for damages. And, the Doors were informed, police would be waiting in the wings with arrest warrants all filled in – all they had to do was write in the charges and arrest Jim on the spot.

'A "fuck clause",' Jim said when he was told about it. 'I bet it's a rock and roll first.'

One of the first big concerts was set for Mexico in June. The Doors were to play the Plaza Monumental, which was Mexico City's biggest bull ring, as its name implied. The idea was to charge only 40 cents to a dollar admission, so the kids of the city could attend. I was the only writer invited to go along (for *Rolling Stone*). I remember visiting the Doors' office the night before scheduled departure. Mario Olmos, the concert pro-moter, arrived at the office with a $20,000 cashier's cheque and told Billy Siddons and the others that the performance wasn't going to be in the bull ring, it was going to be in a large night club comparable to the Copa in New York or the Ambassador Hotel in Los Angeles. Olmos, who brought Javier Castro, the owner of the Forum, with him, said he just hadn't been able to get all the permits necessary. As in America, there had been student riots in Mexico City and the government didn't want that many young people collected in one place at the same time. The Doors had not been consulted about this venue change and they didn't like it.

The small office was lighted by candles, empty beer bottles were scattered around, and everybody was saying things like, 'Fuck it, we won't go.' Mario explained that it wasn't his fault,

On stage, Jim could manipulate the audience with silence.

and it probably wasn't, at least not entirely, and eventually Jim and the others changed their minds and went home to finish packing. The next day we were on a plane with thousands of pounds of sound equipment.

We stayed in a nice motel built around a swimming pool in a nice section of the city, not far from the archaeological museum. (Very classy by Mexico City standards, the guard at the gate had a silver-handled pistol in his holster and a little custom-made waterproof cover for the handle when it rained.) We were given a translator, a bright woman with even more class than the motel had, and a pair of black and white Cadillac limousines were made available 24 hours a day.

After we arrived, Jim asked if I would switch rooms with him, which I did. Later that night, of course, Pam called and the switchboard put her through to me. Which was Jim's plan all along. So I told her she had the wrong room and I gave her the right one and got the switchboard back. Next morning, Jim smiled at me and said, 'You really know how to hurt a guy.'

Jim remained playful throughout the week. The first night he and I shared the white limo, while the other three Doors travelled in the black one. As we approached the club, I saw a fifteen-foot-high painting of Jim's face on the wall of the front of the club. It didn't look like the bearded Jim at all.

The other Doors alighted from the black Cadillac and were greeted by screams from the fans clustered near the stage entrance. No one paid any attention as Jim left our car. He wasn't recognized. He chuckled and called out to the fans, 'Hey! Over here! Give the singer some.'

Before the show, I sat with Billy Siddons at a nearby cafe. Billy told me he was very unhappy about Jim's refusal to shave his beard. He said he had asked Jim to shave, but he refused.

The performances were good and well received. 'The End', as it turned out, was the Doors' biggest hit in Mexico, for reasons that experts in Catholicism and macho lifestyles will have to sort out. When Jim got to the line, 'Father I want to kill you/Mother I want to...,' all the young men in the audience finished the lyric for him, at the top of their voices. We also discovered that the song was a staple in Mexico City juke boxes and usually had been played so frequently, it was worn right down to the white plastic interior.

For the full week, Jim was on his best behaviour. Mainly he stayed by himself, reading. When he did go out, he was approachable, friendly, using his high school Spanish to communicate with the local fans. The day we went to the archaeological museum, he paired off with a young redhead, an American woman who was known to be one of the 'Presidential groupies', the band of mainly American women who had attached themselves to the President's son. Another day, we went to a park where the mariachis performed and Jim and I got drunk together and he paid an extravagant sum for a waiter's wooden serving tray. Still another night, as we were returning to the motel from the club, again he was a little drunk and as the chauffeur pushed the speedometer to 80, slowing to 50 for the right angle turns, Jim leaned out of the limo and pointed his finger like a pistol.

'Andele! (Hurry!),' he shouted into the night. 'Bang . . . bang . . . bang! Andele! Andele!' A bandit riding with Zapata's ghost in a Cadillac along the Avenue de la Revolucion on a sultry Mexican night.

In the year that followed, only a few of the times I saw Jim had anything to do with rock and roll. Now he invited me to poetry readings, and screenings of films he thought I'd enjoy. One of the readings – at which Jim read some of his poems – with Michael McClure – was a fund-raiser for Norman Mailer, who was running for mayor of New York.

Other times we met at Barney's Beanery and drank, talking about writing and writers. I was by now working on an Elvis Presley book for Simon & Schuster – the book that Jim suggested – and we shared the same editor, so we had a common meeting ground. There was a picture taken of Jim during the Miami concert, in his leather hat with the skull and crossbones on the hat band; Jim's eyes were closed and he was bearded. Jim told me that he had told his editor he wanted that photograph on the cover of the book. The editor argued gently for a picture that would be more recognizable. Jim was watching his own poetry move through the editing process.

*Long before the Miami scandal, Jim's performance
style was designed to shock and titillate.*

'He was so serious,' the editor, Jonathan Dolger, told me. 'He'd had so many rejections on his poetry. He wasn't concerned at all with money. We didn't pay him much. He was concerned with the look of the book and with the tastefulness of the way the book was published. It was important that I take him seriously as a writer.

'I found his poetry interesting. Some of it's very bad. I suggested taking some of it out, but he didn't. We changed the order. I made some suggestions. *The Lords* was not so good and I thought we should cut some of that out. He didn't want that particularly, but we did some reorganizing.'

In the late summer and fall of 1989, Jim rented first the second and then the ground floor of a building across the street from the Elektra offices. Babe and Frank and Paul and anyone who had anything to do with the documentary film – still being edited – occupied the second floor space. The ground floor was for Pamela and a boutique she was planning, which eventually cost Jim more than $250,000.

They still fought as passionately as they loved and both continued to spend a lot of time with other sexual partners. One of Jim's long-time drinking friends, Tom Baker, was still around and he remembered that when they went to the rock clubs on the Sunset Strip, 'Morrison was usually in a stupor and seemed oblivious to the fans. As soon as we sat down, the resident groupies would pounce on him. Sometimes I would share in the spoils. Other times I would be ignored as though I were invisible. Still other times Jim would be so comatose I would get them all to myself.

'One night we went to the grim little Hollywood flat of two of these creatures and sat up till dawn drinking and talking. One girl soon revealed herself to be a practising junkie and she brought out a plastic vial of pills, blue tablets called New Morthone, a strong synthetic morphine. We crushed them with a tablespoon and sniffed the powder. The high was speedy and euphoric and Jim became loose and talkative, telling us endless tales about himself, including the story of his body being inhabited by the spirit of an old Indian dying by the side of a New Mexico highway.

'After a while, I went to bed in the front room with the

junkie and the other girl began to wrestle Jim into her bedroom. He had become somewhat inert and sat with his head on the kitchen table. After a great effort, she got him into her bed and shut the door. About ten minutes later, she joined the junkie and me, complaining about Jim's lack of interest. Soon, the three of us were engaged in a robust bout of interchanging sexual positions and then I passed out, exhausted and content.

'I awoke at the crack of noon, alone. I sat in the kitchen drinking instant coffee and smoking cigarettes for about fifteen minutes. Then curiosity got the best of me and I slowly opened the bedroom door and looked in. The little beggars had abandoned me for Jim, and he and the junkie were asleep alongside one another. The other girl was feverishly giving Jim head, trying to pump some life into his pathetically limp dick. She looked not unlike a young lioness feeding on her fallen prey. She glanced over at me for a moment, then went right back to work. I returned to the kitchen and crushed up another pill.'

Pam and Jim took a second-floor apartment in a two-storey building on Norton Avenue, not far from Barney's Beanery. Diane Gardiner, who had stopped doing publicity for the Doors, lived in an apartment downstairs. 'They were amusing neighbours,' Diane told me. 'Also dramatic. They lived a swashbuckling kind of existence. Their stairway came down to my doorway and they'd have fights up and down the stairs, like Errol Flynn. Then Jim would throw his books out the window. The next morning he would pick up his books and move back in again.

'One time Pamela took me to Rive Gauche in Beverly Hills, where she bought $5,000 worth of clothes. She'd run off to the dressing room, hissing at me, "He owes me this! He owes me this!" '

It was never boring. Always, drama was in the room, or in an adjacent one. Jay Sebring, the hair stylist who had shaped Jim's leonine look back in 1967, was one of the people killed with Sharon Tate by Charlie Manson's gang. That was in the late summer of 1969. And that was when the Woodstock generation took one step forward and two steps back. The Woodstock gathering was in August, becoming an instant myth for the decade, and when only a couple of months later, the Rolling Stones hired the Hell's Angels to provide security at a free concert in Altamont, California, and they beat a naked, fat boy to death with pool cues, they symbolically killed everyone.

Elektra was demanding more product, wanted a new album by Christmas. To everyone's amazement, the band produced one of the best of the Doors' career. *Morrison Hotel*, named for a $2.50-a-night hotel in skid row Los Angeles (in front of which the group posed for a photograph), contained a substantial body of fair poetry and some of the band's best blues.

Some of the strongest stuff came from something Ray found in one of Jim's notebooks titled 'Abortion Stories'. This included references to blood running in the streets of Chicago, 'blood in my love in the terrible summer, bloody red sun of Phantastic L.A.'. The title given the song, 'Peace Frog', was ludicrous, but the message was strong. This song also contained Jim's only recorded reference to the much-told story from his childhood, when he witnessed Indians dying along a New Mexico highway.

By now, Jim had bought a cottage for Pam in Topanga Canyon behind a country bar and club, so he wrote a song called 'Roadhouse Blues'. It was one of several songs inspired at least in part by Pamela and the one song that best captured Jim's live-fast-die-young-and-make-a-good-looking-corpse philosophy.

The 'La Cienega symphony' was history and the apocalyptic Doors were back. The singles selected for release from the album, 'Running Blue' and 'You Make Me Real', sold poorly, but *Morrison Hotel* was another major hit, becoming the fifth album in a row to sell more than a million copies. This was a first for an American band.

In November, 1969, Jim flew to Phoenix with Tom Baker to see the Rolling Stones in concert. They were drunk, of course, and en route they started throwing things around the cabin and harassing the flight crew. This led to their being arrested by the FBI upon landing and charged with being drunk and disorderly and interfering with the flight of an aircraft, an offence under the 'skyjacking' law that could lead to a $10,000 fine and a ten-year sentence.

The same month, Jim appeared in Miami in Judge Murray Goodman's courtroom to plead not guilty to the charges that came out of the concert in March. Trial was set for April 1970. In the following months, as Jim and his lawyers spent more and more time planning his defence, and Billy Siddons tried to get the Doors back into the concert halls, Jim tried to get something going in film. His words to Fred Myrow seemed to be echoing in his mind every day: 'If I don't find a new way to develop creatively within a year, I'll be good for nothing but nostalgia.' However much others insisted he continue with his music career, however often he was drunk – and by now it was almost an everyday occurrence – his goal stayed fixed in place, clear, commanding, immutable.

Jim and his friends had completed a short 'feature' called *HWY*. If it left the viewer desiring resolution, it also was a compelling work. On the one hand it was little more than a student's film, impressionistic and deliberately quirky, but it had been filmed slowly and on a comfortable budget, which gave it a sense of professionalism, and with Jim's peculiar mind serving as the engine, it produced a mysterious, almost mystical look into a killer's mind. Jim was virtually the only actor in the film and its director.

He was a hitchhiker in the desert. He got a ride and then, suddenly, the driver of the car was gone and Jim was behind the wheel. What happened to the driver was not explained, only hinted at. In one scene, Jim entered a telephone booth and told someone, 'I wasted him.' (As a practical joke, Jim actually called Michael McClure in the scene, and never explained; all McClure ever heard was Jim saying, 'I wasted him,' then hang up. He figured Jim was drunk and forgot about it.) In the film, Jim then drove into L.A. and there was a lot of footage of bars and cars and cops at night. The movie ended ambiguously.

Over the months that followed, everyone who saw it commented favourably on Jim's presence, or charisma, but thought the film little more than an academic joke; it was, like Jim's film at UCLA, short, without plot, and strange.

On stage in Miami: Jim and Robby Krieger.

Therefore, without commercial potential.

During the same period, Jim met with Timothy Leary to talk about documenting his run for the California governorship, but Leary was thrown into jail, aborting the project. Efforts to make a deal with Carlos Casteneda to film his book, *The Teachings of Don Juan*, were no more successful, and when Steve McQueen considered Jim for a role in a film called *Adam at 6 P.M.*, Jim was rejected because the producers thought his drinking would be a liability.

There were a couple of good concerts in January 1970, followed by meetings with Elektra in New York. A young publicist with Rogers & Cowan, the publicity firm that had represented them from the start, had come up with a new campaign, in which Jim would be promoted as a 'renaissance man'. Poet. Lyricist. Singer. Actor. Director. The memorandum from the company files showed that its author believed it was necessary for Jim to be comfortable with the concept, but it ended with a note that turned Jim off completely: 'There aren't any Leonardos on the scene, and they'll love it in Poughkeepsie.'

The Doors were in New York to perform at the Felt Forum, a concert hall connected to Madison Square Garden. There was a party following the last of four shows, hosted by Elektra Records. The Doors' contract was about to expire and it was typical for record companies in such a situation to show sudden and expensive interest. It was the perfect party, with all the right people, the best food, and a screening of Alfred Hitchcock's *The Thirty-Nine Steps*. On the way out, Pamela, on Jim's arm, told Jac Holzman, 'Well, in case we're on Atlantic next year, thanks for the swell party.' The 'renaissance man' idea was dropped and the Doors renewed their Elektra contract, promising one more album.

The funny thing is, the 'renaissance man' concept wasn't inappropriate, only badly motivated from Jim's point of view – and perhaps a little pretentious. Surely Jim was wise to decline. Living down the Lizard King label was hard enough; he wasn't about to wear DaVinci's cloak.

By late February 1970, Jim had started meeting with Jim Aubry, the one-time programming chief at CBS TV, now between jobs but soon to be president of MGM. After their first meeting, Aubry turned to an assistant and said, 'Jim Morrison's going to be the biggest motion picture star of the next ten years. He's going to be the James Dean of the seventies.' He told his assistant to sign Jim to a contract at any cost and that resulted in an agreement to have Jim work with Michael McClure in turning Michael's unpublished novel, *The Adept*, into a screenplay.

Aubry's assistant was Bill Bellasco, a former agent whose company, St. Regis Films, was the joint venture partner in the project with Jim's company, HiWay Productions. 'Aubry's interest in Jim was in his overall creative abilities,' Belasco told me. 'Jim was co-writing the script with McClure and Jim and I were going to co-produce the film and Jim was going to be the star. Aubry and I had a hunch about Jim that if he could ever be harnessed, he could be a film maker. Whether that meant director, writer, or producer, or a combination, we didn't know. The problem of course was discipline.'

According to Michael McClure, discipline *wasn't* a problem, at least not for as long as he was involved. An office was provided in the 9000 Sunset Building and McClure said they kept regular hours. 'Jim was hung-over and late a few times, I was the same,' he said. 'But generally we started at 9:30, worked until 12:30, took off for an hour, came back and worked until 4:30 or 5:30. This went on for six weeks. We turned out a script that was longer than the novel. It looked like somebody shot the manuscript of *Moby Dick* out of a cannon.'

As the script was being written, Aubry moved into the president's office at MGM and Jim began meeting with directors, including Sam Fuller, a seasoned veteran known mainly for his action B-movies but regarded by some as one of the most influential film makers of the post-war period. He was a hard drinker, too, and while Jim had great respect for his talent, ultimately Fuller was found to be unacceptable by MGM.

Taking his place was Ted Flicker, the young director of the Premise Players, a group of maverick satirists who came to Hollywood in the early 1960s. By 1967, Flicker had written and directed the vastly under-appreciated satire, *The President's Analyst*.

At the same time, Aubry was trying to get Jim to take an acting role in another film while the script was being completed. Jim read several scripts, but turned them down. Today, McClure thinks the screenwriting assignment was merely 'a way for Jim to get into the movies. We all got what we wanted. Belasco was doing his producer bit, Aubry thought he was getting Jim as an actor, and we were learning how to write a film script and thought we were into a real project.'

As Belasco remembered it, the film began to fall apart by mid-summer. The script, now called *St Nicholas*, named for the major character, a dope dealer, had been cut from 'something two inches thick to 90 flimsy pages. I was there when it was cut. The winnowing down was done in two days. Winnowing down? It was an amputation.'

The Doors were another hospital case. While Billy Siddons was now able to find them more bookings, everyone I talked to agreed that the relationship between Jim and the others was strained.

Belasco said, 'The conflict grew out of the Miami incident, for which they all held Jim responsible and they'd begun to do numbers in their own heads that he had ruined their careers. Which I always resented, because they wouldn't have had careers if it hadn't been for Jim Morrison. So he was carrying the whole burden on his back. And they were making it uncomfortable for him. However irresponsible Jim may have been, they had a responsibility to him, because he made the group. They knew going in he was not responsible by their standards. When the money was rolling in, nobody complained. When things went wrong, caused by that same frenetic personality that made things right earlier, everybody ran away.'

Aubry among others tried to convince Jim to leave the band. It was no secret that Atlantic Records wanted him. MGM Records also wanted Jim, alone, and Belasco tried to

*Moments after the infamous Miami concert ends,
Morrison emerges from his dressing room to stare
down trance-like at the chaos below.*

talk him into making the move. 'He could've made millions alone,' Bellasco said. But Jim refused to act. Though he may not have had anything other than his livelihood in common with the other three members of the group, he remained loyal.

One reason may have been that he needed the money. Much of 1970 was devoted not to film, or music, but to jurisprudence and his lawyer, Max Fink, was not cheap; people in the Doors camp told me that the Miami trial probably cost Jim a half a million dollars.

The Phoenix trial in March was another cost. Jim was clean-shaven now and, like Tom Baker, dressed neatly in a white shirt. One of the stewardesses said she had been mauled by one of the defendants, but 'the girls had Jim and me confused,' Baker said. 'Everyone else who testified, including the other government witnessses, contradicted them, but the judge accepted their word along with the claim that Jim made an obscene gesture toward Sherry Ann and uttered the "pussy" word. So, based on the cockamamie testimony of these two airheads, Jim was convicted of a misdemeanour, and I was totally acquitted. Jim was confused, because if anyone made a move, it was done by whoever was sitting in my seat.'

That night, Jim and Baker got drunk with the Phoenix lawyer who had joined Max Fink in the defence. They 'started talking about calling Sherry Ann and her friend. The lawyer could not believe we would have anything to do with them after they tried to put us in jail. I told him we were really going to get back at them by taking them out into the desert and fucking them and leaving them there. Jim and I exchanged broad winks, then he said not only would we strip them and fuck them, but we would urinate on their bare bodies before deserting them. The lawyer was cockeyed drunk and crawling around on his hands and knees, pleading with us not to do it. He looked pathetic and we laughed at him and tormented him until he passed out.'

The party continued in Los Angeles when they returned, concluding the following night with Jim and Tom punching it out in the Doors' office. Jim ended up calling the sheriff's office on Tom and when they came, seeing who was involved, they told the boys to go home and sleep it off. Later that night,

Tom heaved a rock through the Doors' office window. Jim did not speak for Tom for the next eight months.

The Miami trial was traumatic in a much different way. Max Fink prepared a 63-page document worthy of publication in a legal journal, connecting dozens of legal cases involving films such as *I Am Curious, Yellow* and *Midnight Cowboy*, the art of Gauguin and Michelangelo, and the First, Eighth and Fourteenth Amendments to the Constitution. Of the four laws that Jim was charged with breaking, the most recent had been enacted in 1918, and Max and Jim fully expected to be able to introduce the concept of 'contemporary community standards'. Max wanted jurors to be able to see *Hair* and some of the comedians performing in Miami's clubs.

They were wrong. In August, when the trial began, Judge Hoffman was getting ready for a tough re-election campaign in the fall and it appeared that Jim's trial was a part of his campaign. All of Max's petitions were denied and the 63-page brief was disregarded.

Harvey Perr was a young playwright who worked from time to time for Elektra as a publicist. After listening to the tapes of the Miami concert, he believed that Jim's performance had been a statement.

'It was very rhythmic,' he told me. 'I mean, for all the obscenity, he was really telling the audience to revolt, to revolt against the overpriced tickets, to revolt against the system, and to love each other. He said: "Fuck your neighbour, fuck your neighbour." It all had a rhythm, almost like one of his poems. It was like this big, brawling, drunken poem, telling them to revolt. And it really seemed to me to come out of that spirit that he had got at the Living Theatre. I mentioned that to him and he thought that was very perceptive. It was I think very important for him that he was doing something very consciously from the beginning that he felt was revolutionary. Once the judge denied all of Max's motions, Jim wasn't interested any more.'

Mike Gershman, the Doors' first publicist, who hadn't represented the group in some time, was employed to handle the trial press. The thing that surprised him was that the national press was about as interested in covering the trial

```
                                              I.   LEWD AND LASCIVIOUS
                                                   BEHAVIOR (FEL)
                                             II.   INDECENT EXPOSURE (MISD)
                                            III.   OPEN PROFANITY    (MISD)
TO:    THE DADE COUNTY SHERIFF'S OFFICE     CHARGE IV.   DRUNKENNESS (MISD)

_____ Defendant ___ TO BE ARRESTED ___

JAMES MORRISON                                      69- 2355
        Name of Defendant

Address                          Phone      Race __W__  Sex __M__  Age _____

                                            Height _____ Weight _____
Business Address                 Phone
       Member of musical group
       (The Doors)                          Hair _____ Eyes _____
              Occupation or Business

       3/1/69        Dinner Key Auditorium  Complexion _____
Date of Offense      Location of Offense    Marks or
                                            Features
REMARKS: Booking Agent for "The Doors" is   Comments

       Ashley Famous Agency, 1301 Ave. of the                FILED
                                                           MAR 5 1969
       Americas, New York City, New York                 J. F. McCRACKEN
Complainant (s) (Note: If filed by an officer, both the name of the victim and of the department are shown below CLERK

       Bob Jennings, 495 NW 93rd St.
Name   Theodore Seaman, MPD         Address                              Phone

ASSISTANT STATE ATTORNEY: _____ ALFONSO C. SEPE  alc

201.01-5
```

A copy of the warrant for Jim's arrest issued by
Dade County Sheriff's office, 1969. He was
accused of lewd and lascivious behaviour, indecent
exposure, open profanity and drunkenness.

as the judge was interested in hearing Max's arguments.

'So here we go to Miami to what could and should have been a very pivotal political trial and at the time as a publicist, I remember banging my head against the wall, writing to all the *Times* and *Newsweeks* and so on about coverage, and *Rolling Stone* and all the rock papers and everybody. And nobody was interested. I wrote a series of articles for *Rock* magazine. One was called 'Apathy for the Devil' [a play on the title of the Rolling Stones' recent album, *Sympathy for the Devil*] which put it into perspective. Woodstock had happened the previous year. To me, the exposure was a tremendously political issue and I couldn't get through to people, to make them understand it. I was in Miami for three weeks for the trial.

Morrison stands outside the Miami courtroom
after being sentenced to 6 months in jail and fined
$500 for indecent exposure and public profanity,
October 1970.

Gloria Vanjeck did a piece for *Stone*. I did the series for *Rock*. But that was it.'

There was another disappointment for Jim. Not even his local fans supported him. 'The trial was "the afternoon of a superstar,"' Gershman said. 'The first day, a hundred kids showed up at nine in the morning. Second day it was forty. Third day it was twelve.'

It also appeared that Jim was being railroaded. If Phoenix had been odd, Miami was no less than bizarre. One day, the prosecutor brought a Doors album into the courtroom and asked Jim to autograph it. Another day, he handed Jim a piece of paper on which he had written a limerick:

'There once was a group called the Doors
Who sang in dissent of the mores
To youth they protested
As witnesses attested
While the leader was dropping his drawers.'

The prosecution's witnesses were ludicrous. They present-ed a picture of chaste and offended middle-America, a perfect follow-up to the Orange Bowl rally against indecency that had followed the concert, a comforting, flag-waving vehicle for the judge's re-election campaign. Teenagers in pony-tails testified as to how shocked they were by Jim's performance and moth-ers of those teenagers spluttered their indignation. There were seventeen witnesses in all and virtually every one of them either worked in or was related to someone who worked in the prosecutor's office or for the police department.

Midway through the trial, the prosecution offered a deal. Said Gershman, 'If Jim would do a free concert, not at the Orange Bowl, because they had the decency rally, if he gave a concert, at Brandon Park, I think, and gave the proceeds to their anti-drug thing in Miami, the City's drug abuse pro-gramme, they'd drop everything except one misdemeanour, which would mean a suspended sentence. I guess it was drunkenness or abusive language. The deal was considered for a couple of days and turned down.'

Jim sat calmly through it all, drawing pictures of the wit-nesses in his notebook. With the jury out of the courtroom, Max Fink made a final, passionate plea to have 'contemporary community standards' introduced as part of the defence, mak-ing a half-hour speech in support of free speech, but the judge ruled again to deny.

When Max called his witnesses, no one in the jury seemed to be showing much interest. All experts in censorship and free speech were disallowed and those who survived the chal-lenge from the bench really had little to say, except that they hadn't seen Jim expose himself.

There was one other small drama not told until now. During the trial, the judge went to a restaurant and was ques-tioned about the case by friends with whom he was dining.

Mike Gershman said, 'A girl overheard the judge say, "Don't worry about it, we're going to throw him in jail," or words to that effect. "We're going to get him." One of the local attorneys found out who the girl was and it turned out she was an entertainer. I was sent to talk to the girl, to see if she would testify about what she overheard in the restaurant, because this was grounds for a mistrial, because the judge cannot go around saying somebody is guilty before the trial's over. She was at the airport on her way to Las Vegas. I rushed to the airport, found her, she said she wasn't interested, didn't want to get involved. I had been told to make a pitch other than money or morality, and what'd that leave? I asked, "Want to meet Jim Morrison?" She said no, got on the plane, and that's the last we saw of her.'

When the verdict was finally read, Jim put down the book he was reading, a biography of Jack London, and looked without emotion at the judge. He had been found guilty of exposure and profanity. On all other charges, including drunkenness, he was found innocent. Bail was set, a date was scheduled for sentencing, and Jim returned to Los Angeles.

Said Mike Gershman, 'The last time we talked was about a book called *The Last Strange Voyage of Donald Crowhurst*, an amazing book. The trial wasn't over and we all knew he was going to be found guilty of something. The book's about a guy in a boat race and he's the first person to travel thousands of miles and reach a set point. Well, Donald Crowhurst decides to take a shortcut, rather than go the prescribed distance, and he alters his log and he wins. But he cracks up because the winning becomes paramount and he does the deceitful thing and is so appalled with himself that he goes stark raving crazy. I knew the book and Jim had just read it. Jim had tremendous empathy for this guy. Jim knew the trial was really over and that his career was really over, no matter what remained to be done.'

In September Jim told Salli Stevenson of *Circus* magazine that the Miami concert was his declaration of independence. The audience was there not to listen to music, but to see him do something outrageous, and he was telling them to wake up. His image had gotten out of hand, he said, and however

responsible he was for that happening, he was 'fed up'. He had lived a couple of lifetimes in just a few years, he added, and if he had to go to jail, he hoped the other three Doors would continue as an instrumental trio. And if he had it to do over, he would do it differently: rather than be the Roman candle, he would go for the 'quiet, demonstrative artist-plodding-in-his-own-garden trip'.

Jim returned to Miami the end of October, just a week before election time. The judge delivered a campaign speech, telling Jim, 'the suggestion that your conduct was acceptable by community standards is just not true. To admit that this nation accepts as a community standard the indecent exposure and the offensive language spoken by you would be to admit that a small minority who spew obscenities, who disregard law and order, and who display utter contempt for our institutions and heritage have determined the community standards for all.'

For exposure and profanity, Jim was given the maximum: a fine of $500 and six months in Raiford Prison, widely recognized as one of the nation's nastiest.

Jim's personal life was equally turbulent. Early in the year, he sent his poetry books to and then started corresponding with Patricia Kennealy, the magazine editor he had met in New York following the Madison Square Garden show. Patricia liked some of the poetry and reviewed it intelligently in her magazine, *Jazz & Pop*. Patricia told me that it was well short of a rave review, but apparently Jim was impressed. He sent her a telegram saying, 'Thanks for the pat on the back' and later told her, 'It was the first time anyone'd reviewed his work and not him.'

The relationship was spotty, like most with Jim (including Pamela's). Their times together were infrequent and rather ordinary; they went to see a couple of movies together (something by Ingmar Bergman; Mick Jagger's *Ned Kelly*), they sat in the lighting booth with Allen Ginsberg to watch the

Jim Morrison and Pamela Courson. Pamela stood by him to the end.

143

Jefferson Airplane in concert, they went shopping for books, they went for a walk in Central Park. More unusual, Jim corresponded with Patricia, sending her 'notes on steno pads, four or five pages, one or two words to a line, only four or five lines to a page.

'He said he used to practice his signature a lot,' Patricia said. 'He was proud of it. He'd decided at an early age what it was going to look like, with the "J" and the "M" stuck together. It was very studied.'

Jim was intrigued. The books they bought together revealed a shared intelligence. Jim bought a 'copy of Shakespeare's sonnets, lots of Petrarch, *The Thousand Songs of Mila Rape*, the airplane poems of Allen Ginsberg . . . ' and Patricia gave him a book by Robert Graves called *Watch the North Wind Rise*, 'because he was interested in the occult at that time. I'd just told him I was a witch and he wanted to know everything. I reduced it to its most basic terms. I said it was a pagan mother-worship and he thought that was absolutely terrific, goddess rather than god worship, so I gave him a couple of books to read. '

They made love in June 1970 and were 'married' on June 24th in Patricia's Lower East Side apartment in a witch's ceremony. Standing in candle light before a high priestess of Patricia's coven, they both pricked their hands, dropping blood into a glass of wine, which they then shared. A drop of blood was affixed to the certificate which Jim signed in huge script 'JMorrison'. Patricia said that was when Jim fainted.

About two months later, mid-way through the trial in Miami, Patricia called and then went to Miami, saying she was pregnant and what was Jim going to do? Initially, Jim avoided Patricia, and when he finally agreed to meet her he was, by turns, compassionate, evasive, and coy.

She said, 'I'm sorry, I know it 's a bad time and you're hung up with the trial, but I don't like this any more than you do and it was your fault, you did a dumb thing and pulled out my diaphragm, and we're just gonna have to do something about it.' He acknowledged that the child probably was his, said he didn't want to be a father, or married, offered to pay for an abortion and promised to hold her hand during the operation, and then said, shyly, 'You know, it'd really be an incredible kid.'

Patricia said, 'Yeah, but I don't think that's any reason to have the kid. You just don't see if two terrific people can turn out a terrific product together. You don't really care for kids that much in the first place. What'd I do with it? I mean, the only reason I'd have it would be because it was yours, and I don't think that's any reason to have the child.'

Jim said, 'You know, this subject has never come up before.'

Patricia said, 'Don't give me that bullshit, I know it has.'

He said, 'No, no, never. This is the first time.'

Patricia decided to hell with it and they went off to the hotel bar and got drunk.

Jim was not present in November when Patricia had her abortion. By then he was in a tailspin. Billy Siddons and the Doors' agents were lining up fewer and fewer concerts and on top of that, it continued difficult to get Jim into a studio to record new material. That was one of the reasons for assembling *Absolutely Live*, the double album that was recorded over a period of more than six months and released in July. Live albums had been successful for several bands in 1969 and it was regarded as an easy way for a band to satisfy a contractual obligation to produce an agreed-upon number of albums in an agreed length of time. In the Doors' case, it also took up the slack in unfertile times.

Paul Rothchild, the producer who had been with the Doors from the start, hated the album. He said, 'It shouldn't have been made and shouldn't have been released. It should have been made as a movie. It was difficult to convey the Doors live on tape. The Doors' albums were overstatement from the very first, in much the same way that a Shakespearean actor must overstate his lines to reach the back of the theatre. You couldn't do a straight recording of the Doors and succeed after the first album. It required a ten to one ratio, which is a low recovery average.

'The Doors were not great live performers musically. They were exciting theatrically and kinetically, but as musicians they didn't make it, there was too much inconsistency, there was too much bad music. Robby would be horrendously out

145

of tune with Ray, John would be missing cues, there was bad mike usage too where you couldn't hear Jim at all. As a movie it still would've worked.

'It shouldn't have been released because live albums were a drug on the market by then. The public had tired of them. But the general consensus in the industry among the top people was live LPs were a great way to catch another album from a group having a slow time recording and to catch the peak of a buying wave. It was logical, but the music market didn't go for it. Jac Holzman even insisted the album sell for $11.90 – the equivalent of two $5.95 records. We were hoping at the worst it'd sell for $6.95 and then wouldn't be a drug on the market. It turned out to be the worst disaster the Doors ever had, saleswise.'

When more time went by without any promise of new material, Elektra Records began planning its first repackaging of old hits, which became 13, a collection of thirteen previously recorded songs, including all the hits. (The official line at Elektra was that there were thirteen songs because the most anyone included on an album during this period was twelve – with the number declining fast – and, thus, thirteen was a bargain. Others said that the title was connected to the highly publicized fact that the thirteenth letter in the alphabet was M, which stood for Marijuana. As bizarre as this argument may sound today, it was not strange in 1970; many record buyers wore an 'M' or '13' patch on their jackets.) The record was released in November, the same month Patricia had her abortion.

By now, Pam was heavily into heroin. At first, she merely toyed with it, when it was offered by some of her one-night dates. Now there were binges. Eve Babitz, who had taken Jim to bed when the group was just getting started and now eaked out a living designing album covers, remained a part of the same L.A. rock scene; her sister had made some of Jim's leather suits and Eve drank in the same bars with Jim. Eve said about Pam, 'Everything a nerd could possibly wish to be, Pamela was. She had drugs, took heroin, and was fearless in every situation. Socially she didn't care, emotionally she was shockproof, and as for her eating disorders – her idea of the

Jim and Pam with their dog, Sage.

diet to be on while Jim was in Miami going to court was ten days of heroin. Every time she awoke she did some, so she just sort of slept through her fast.'

Jim was back to drugs as well. Jim had gotten involved with the wife of a film maker he had met while making *HWY*. Call her Magda. The publisher of *No One Here Gets Out Alive* changed her name for legal reasons and I'll change it again. It doesn't matter. Magda was one of Jim's cocaine girls.

Jim started using coke early in the year, during the period when he was meeting with MGM and writing his screenplay with Michael McClure. At one point he gave one of his film contacts an ounce of the stuff and told him to hold on to it and not to give him more than a gram at a time, no matter what he said. Jim loved coke in the same way he enjoyed his earlier drugs, and he went at it in the same unbridled manner. Echoing a famous mountain climber's reason for scaling Mount Everest, he told a friend, 'If there was a mountain of coke in the yard I'd do it up . . . because it was there.'

'I never had coke before,' Magda told me. 'I was a hyped-up person anyway and on coke, watch out! He liked that. He knew when my husband was going to Mexico and at eleven that night the doorbell rang.

'"Who is it?'

'"Jimmy."

'"Which Jimmy?" I opened the door a crack and he put his foot in so I couldn't close it.

'We really got it on. Neither of us was expecting it. He really loved life, and so did I. The only bad thing was there was too much cocaine, which blew our minds. He was trying to live a hundred years in one – going to restaurants and ordering all kinds of food, like for ten people and eating a little bit of everything, or nothing at all. He wanted to try everything, I guess. He thought I was crazier than he was and he wanted to see how far I'd go. And he supplied the coke, a jar of it, with champagne and stuff. And we'd get more crazy and crazy every day until one day there was this really frightening scene.

'One evening he came home and he had all this coke and we had almost all of it and all the champagne and everything.

He learned that I freak out real bad . . . I like to have . . . sometimes, I, you know, drink blood, for instance . . . being from Transylvania. And he said, "Well, why don't we drink some blood?"

'I got some dirty razor blades and cut myself. He didn't dare to cut himself because he was scared of any pain. So I started cutting away, all these cuts. Because the blood didn't come at first.'

Magda showed me the backs of her hands. There were eight or ten half-inch scars on each, at the base of her thumbs.

'And suddenly it came and we just had blood all over the place and freaked out and danced in the moonshine,' she said. 'Just wheeeeeewwwww-eeee-ooooooo. And after that we just got very scared where it can go, you know, because the mornings after these freakouts are really sad. Waking up and all these pools of blood . . . '

Jim had moved into the Château Marmont, the hotel where, years later, John Belushi overdosed. In 1970, it was still known mainly as a temporary home for visiting actors from New York, but the rock and rollers were making it their home, as well. I visited there earlier in the year to interview the singer-songwriter Tim Hardin. Jim came by the same day and sat quietly against a wall for several hours, just watching the scene. Tim, who was a heroin addict, went into the bathroom at some point and shot up, leaving the sink and mirror and wall splattered with his blood for all to see. When Jim moved into one of the cottages near the pool at the end of 1970, the hotel's reputation was still going down.

A film writer named Larry Marcus visited him there several times. He had presented a story line to Jim during the Miami trial about a rock singer who'd committed a 'public disgrace at the Albert Hall in London'. Marcus said it was based on Jim's own story and, predictably, Jim hated the idea.

Over the next six months they discussed several other ideas. 'We came up with a motherfucker of an idea, a marvellous film that we had to do, with a human being who wanted to vanish from the world and become zero,' Marcus said. 'The hero was to have nothing to do with music. He insisted upon that. The hero he most liked was a Los Angeles film editor.

The suggestion of doing anything about Jim as a singer was over, to his great relief, because he could then put so much of himself into the character who was not a singer, and as he talked about that character, it was Jim again. It was Jim who was married and had kids and left it all behind because in his desperate search – in his frantic search for zero. Those were Jim's exact words: "frantic search for zero." The film editor went to Mexico for a few days and kept on going. Ultimately the man was in a jungle in which no one else lived, alone. I had a feeling that was a very crucial metaphor for how he felt about himself.

'I got money for the film – like that!' Marcus snapped his fingers. 'From Fred Weintraub, who had produced a couple of films at that time, including *Woodstock*. All Fred wanted was absolute living proof that Jim would do the film and he'd go with the money. We were going to co-write, co-produce, and co-direct, Jim and Larry . . . '

It ended badly one night when Marcus and Frank Lisciandro and Jim went to dinner on the Sunset Strip. Jim drank an entire bottle of scotch and verbally destroyed Marcus's story line, ridiculing it, and him, just before going out onto Sunset Boulevard to direct traffic with his coat as if the passing BMWs and Corvettes were bulls.

Soon after that, on his 27th birthday, December 8th, Jim said he wanted to record some of his poetry. The engineer who had worked his early recordings with the Doors, John Haeny, booked Village Recorders in West Los Angeles, near the bar where Jim had done much of his heavy drinking during his days at UCLA. Haeny brought a bottle of Bushmill's Irish whisky and gave it to Jim. Jim drank it as he read his poetry. Haeny walked away at the end of the evening with six hours of tape, most of it unusable because of Jim's drunkenness. Jim's friends, who had accompanied him to the studio, walked away with Jim unconscious, carrying him by his arms and legs.

Haeny told me he had, maybe, eighty minutes of usable poetry and with that, he signed a letter of agreement with Jim the last day of December 1970 to produce an album of poetry, to be released by Elektra.

At the same time, Jim and the other Doors decided to record what became their final album together. Though the band had been through hard times, rarely working together and talking together only a little more, they had managed to plan some songs. Jim brought in some poetry and they worked together in the rehearsal studio, set up in the ground floor room of the Doors office building.

The band played the songs for Paul Rothchild, who hated them. 'It was awful,' he told me. 'The material was bad, the attitude was bad, the performance was bad. After three days of listening, I said, "That's it!" on the talk-back, cancelled the session, went in and talked to them for three straight hours.

'I said, "Look, I think it sucks, I don't think the world wants to hear it, it's the first time I've ever been bored in a recording studio in my life, I want to go to sleep. The tensions between you guys are phenomenal." I said, "Jim, this is your record. This is the record you have wanted, so you got to get it together. Why don't you guys produce it yourself? I'm gonna drop out." They all came to rely on me getting it to happen so much that I'd found myself becoming more of a cop than a producer. I won't do that in a studio. If the lead singer doesn't want to show up for a session, I don't either.'

The Doors were disappointed and angry, but they believed in the material and decided to take Paul's advice and record the songs themselves. They asked Bruce Botnick, their old engineer, to assist and all agreed to use the Doors' rehearsal room as the studio and the small rest room upstairs as the vocal booth. The result was *L.A. Woman*, an album that was regarded, critically, as one of their two or three best.

One of the longest and ultimately most popular songs on the album was 'Riders On The Storm', a song that started out with the sound of rainfall. Paul Rothchild thought it sounded like 'cocktail lounge music' – at the time, many chi-chi cocktail lounges had fake thunderstorms and the sound of rain as part of the backdrop to the martinis served – and he was equally disparaging about the song that was released as the first single from the album, 'Love Her Madly,' a typical Doors love song.

This does the album an injustice. 'Riders On The Storm' was one of the best tracks, in fact; despite some terrible imagery and banal rhyming, it still managed to be compelling. Arguably the best track was the title song, 'L.A. Woman', Jim's farewell to Los Angeles. And, reminiscent of some earlier blues covers, Jim sang 'Crawling King Snake,' a classic by John Lee Hooker.

More than ever, Jim was walking the streets of West Los Angeles, a hulking, overweight man, bearded, wearing jeans and a rumpled Army fatigue jacket, walking, walking, walking, as if trying to burn the images of the tarnished neighbourhood between Sunset and Santa Monica Boulevards indelibly into his whisky and beer-soaked brain.

Past the Doors' office and the Elektra studios. Past the building where Pamela had her unsuccessful boutique and he had his unproductive film offices. Past the Phone Booth and the Palms and Barney's and all the other cheap bars where he usually stopped for a while to drink. Past Jerry Lewis' and Dean Martin's old clubs and the Playboy Club and the Body Shop (a strip joint) on the Sunset Strip. Past the fashion showroom on Santa Monica Boulevard where Rudi Gernriech designed and introduced the topless bathing suit. Past motorcycle shops and antique stores and every kind of restaurant you can imagine. Past the hundreds of low-rise, stucco apartment buildings, anonymously lined up behind thirsty-looking palm trees, looking tired in the constant smog.

Jim and Pamela still lived on the second floor in one of those apartment buildings, on Norton Avenue, and Diane Gardiner remained downstairs. Between them, and their weird friends, it was like a strange situation comedy, of the sort that David Lynch would like, or maybe Martin Scorcese. Jim was still throwing his books out of the window during evening fights and collecting them in the morning.

Patricia Kennealy told me that in December, 1970, about a month after the abortion, she flew to Los Angeles and left a message at the Doors' office for Jim, fastened to his desk with

Jim on stage in January 1970 at the Felt Forum, a
concert hall attached to Madison Square Garden,
New York.

a knife. She then moved into Diane's apartment. 'Jim called half an hour later,' Patricia said. 'Pam was upstairs at the time. The Doors were recording [*L.A. Woman*] and he asked me to the session. I said recording sessions bore me, why not come here? He said okay and didn't show. I didn't hear from him for three or four days.

'I was at home alone, the phone rings, and it's some girl calling for Pam. Jim and Pam didn't have a phone. So I got Pam and I said, "I met you once, at the Hilton in New York, we had dinner with some other people." Pam was really stoned and she said, "Yeah, whatever happened to that chick, Pat Kennedy . . . Pat Connolly . . . ?" I said, "Pamela, that's me." We talked for three hours, we got stoned and drunk and things got said. There were no ill feelings. It was very lovely and very weird. She told me she wasn't married to Jim and I told her about the baby. I didn't really want to hurt her, but we were smashed and everything just came out. We'd had six joints.

'She said, "Oh, wow, that's so beautiful, but it would've been more beautiful if you could've loved Jim enough to have the baby." That pissed me off. I said, "I loved Jim and I love myself and I loved the kid enough not to have the baby, you know." She said, "Yeah, but if you'd a had the kid, you could a gone away and lived in the country. Of course Jim never would a sent you any money, because that's the way he is . . . "'

At this point, Jim came up the walk. Pamela went 'dead white and rushed out to Jim, pleading, "Jim, Jim, don't look in there . . . it's only Diane."'

Jim laughed and entered the apartment and after a while, and some wine, they started playing the card game War. Jim won the first fifteen or twenty hands and after a while Pamela tried to get Jim to go upstairs with her. He refused.

'Finally, Diane gave Pamela some amyl nitrate and took her upstairs,' Patricia said. 'Jim had a room at the Château and he said he wanted to go there. Then he changed his mind and said he was too drunk to drive, he wanted to stay there. I said, "Here? Where are we going to sleep? On the floor?" He said, "Yeah," and started taking his clothes off. I got a quilt off

Diane's bed and wrapped us up in it and we went to sleep.

'At ten the next morning, Pamela came downstairs, and came to the door. I was cringing. Diane came out of the bedroom, opened the door, said, "I'm not gonna deny he's here." Pamela came in, stood over us. It was like some bad French bedroom farce. It was so ludicrous, so horrible and so funny all at once, no one knew whether to laugh or cry or kill each other.

'Pamela said, "I have only one thing to say to you and I'm gonna say it in front of all these people: 'Jim, you've ruined my Christmas. You spoil it for me every year. This is the fourth year. I just can't stand it any more."

'I said, "Pamela, it isn't what it seems to be, it's perfectly innocent, let me explain . . . "

'And Diane says, "Pamela, what you need is some vitamin pills and some orange juice, come out to the kitchen with me and . . . come on, come on." We get up and Jim's bitching, "Oh, my god, I'll never hear the end of this." I said, "Jim, you wanted it to happen. It was your idea to stay here." He said, "Yeah, yeah, you're always right."

'Pamela came out of the kitchen and we all sat around drinking more wine. I finally reached over and put my arm around her and said, "Pamela, it's all in the family, don't worry about it".

'A month later Patricia paid another visit to California, staying this time with other friends into February, when a major earthquake hit Los Angeles. 'I was panicked, frightened to death,' Patricia told me. 'There were predictions of the city's doom. A full moon. An eclipse. It was all happening that Thursday night. I went to a recording session with my girlfriend with whom I had been staying and she made a play for Jim. I said, "Oh, that's a no-no, wait until I leave. I don't care what you do, but not in front of me, please."

'Because I didn't care what Jim did. He was the complete polygamist. But she was really drunk and Jim was easily lured away. She went to the john and five minutes later Jim left. I found them embracing outside on the lawn. I walked over and said, "Get up!" Jim was smiling, he thought it was funny. I said, "Come on up, both of you, up!"

'So the girl reaches up and pulls me down. My inclination is somewhere between group grope and mayhem. I said, "Let me talk to him by myself." She went away.

'And he said, "Listen, you know I'm too drunk to screw tonight, just let me sleep with her."

'I said, "Look, it's my last night in L.A., I'm going home tomorrow and I'll probably never see you again . . . "

'He said, "Well, I'm not gonna spend another night with you."

'I said, "Okay with me, but you're damned well not going to spend it with her, either." He got disgusted and went inside and she came over and I said, "I'm gonna break your fucking neck." She said, "Don't hurt me, don't hurt me, it's not my fault." Then we went to a topless place, the Phone Booth, where Jim tells her I'm a frustrated lesbian and I go bananas, absolutely bananas.

'We went back to her house and and had a scene in the bathroom where I told her to cool it and she said, "Well, you've always known how fond I was of him." I said, "You fuck, you always told me it was Kris Kristofferson you were after." She pushed me backward and I fell into the bathtub. I got out of the tub, grabbed her by her hair and slammed her into the side of the sink and was going for her eyes when Morrison came in, saying, "Nowwwwwww, ladies . . . "

'We left the bathroom and Jim started going through all the drawers in the apartment. We asked him what he was looking for and he said, "Oh, I'm looking for knives and scissors, so you can't castrate me." We were flabbergasted, we didn't know what to do, so we watched him gather up all the sharp things in the house and put them under the couch. Then he laid on the couch and said he didn't think he had anything to do with the whole thing, he said he thought it was between us two. And then he passed out.

'She suggested we go outside to talk, so we wouldn't wake him up, then proposed we share him, so we could keep him from the groupies and those who didn't really care for him. I saw red. I've never been that angry. It was like looking through red cellophane. I screamed, "YOU FUCKING BITCH, I'M GOING TO KILL YOU!" I grabbed her, threw her down the stairs, gave her a couple of punches, threw her up against the wall, and she said, "I don't want to fight you . . . "

'I said, "FIGHT, YOU FUCKING CUNT OR I'LL KILL YOU!" So she gave me a powderpuff punch and I went into a real rage, giving her a karate number with my foot in her stomach, then I started punching her in the face, and finally I went away, just like that. It was over and I was drained. I told her to take me to the airport and I got on a plane to New York that morning.'

I've devoted far more space to this incident that it deserves, except that it was typical. This is what Jim's life was like, and had been like, from the time he left UCLA through his final days in Los Angeles four years later. I didn't see him much during this period. Occasionally we'd run into each other at one of the bars. But I heard from mutual friends about various scenes that weren't all that different from this one. He was rolling along, drunk much of the time, putting himself out there, pretty much letting life happen to him.

VI

THE EXILE

PAM WAS THE FIRST to talk about Paris. According to Diane Gardiner, she fell in love with a French count, variously identified as Jaime de Bretaille and Jean DeBretti. For more than a year, they had been sharing heroin along with fantasies.

'Pam was fascinated by the idea of royalty,' Diane told me. 'Now, I don't know if he really was a count, but Pam and Jim were fighting and she told me, "The time has come. I've outgrown Jim and it's time to move on. I have this French count who is just dying to be with me." She talked about him all the time. He was so very rich. He and his friends were terribly bored and they took a lot of heroin. He'd tell her, "We're the last of the dinosaurs" – the aristocracy was dying out.'

Jim showed an interest in Paris as well. Some of his friends had lived there and they shared with him their love of the city. After all these years, Jim remained enamoured of many French poets and novelists. With its long, rich tradition of literary exiles, it seemed to offer Jim a comfortable escape hatch, a refuge, a place in which to relax and regroup.

Pam left California first and Jim followed, after spending a few days with Babe. As I look back, I think Babe probably was Jim's closest friend, perhaps the only one who accepted Jim unconditionally, who wanted nothing in return. They shot pool on the Strip and went to Catalina in a boat the Doors had purchased. They went to the Muhammed Ali-Joe Frazier fight. They drank. Jim flew to Paris in early March.

At first, Paris seemed to deliver what Jim wanted, or at least a huge chunk of it. After spending a couple of weeks in a small hotel, they subleased a large, airy apartment in a nice district near the Bastille and in the weeks following Jim wandered the city, visiting museums, tracking down the homes and haunts of his literary heroes, stopping at the sidewalk cafés. Jim and Pam – whose count by now had left Paris – drove to the south of France and into Spain, then took a ship to Tangier, where they rented another car and drove to Casablanca. Another time, they spent a week in Corsica. Jim went to the theatre. He developed a friendship with two French film makers, Agnes Varda and her husband Jacques Demy. (Demy was best known outside France for directing *Umbrellas of Cherbourg* and she was acknowledged as the 'grandmother of New Wave cinema'.) Jim shaved off his beard and lost some weight. He started wearing khaki slacks and crew-neck sweaters, looking very much like an ageing college student. For four months, there were no major incidents.

There were, of course, many small ones. Despite what Pam would say later, Jim continued to drink heavily. In Los Angeles, Jim sometimes had to walk for a few blocks between bars; in Paris, the romantic bistros and sidewalk cafés were everywhere. Paris also offered some sleazy rock and roll clubs of the sort he had loved in Los Angeles. Frequently, Jim found himself going home with people he met along the way. Often, he was drunk for days at a time.

Friends told me that when he called California – rarely – and was told that the critics loved the new album and that it was selling well, he was excited. He told John Densmore that he was writing again and the material was the best he'd ever done – apparently a lie, based on what others said and entries in a fragmentary journal he had begun to keep. He told some of the people he met in Paris that he was writing an opera. The truth is, he spent hours sitting with his notebooks open in front of him, staring for hours at the blank page without writing a word.

Jim tried 'automatic writing', letting his mind empty, hoping that something would be created freely and spontaneously. He tried discipline, sitting down at the desk each day at the same time. He actually hired a secretary, a young American, Robin Wertle, who was fluent in French. Nothing worked.

He got depressed. Enormously depressed, said one friend who saw him in the the final days. By mid-June 1971, his

French friend from Los Angeles, Alain Ronay, was living in the flat with Jim and Pam. At the end of the month he moved into the home of Agnes Varda and Jacques Demy, but stayed in touch. Years later, Ronay revealed that on July 2nd he spent much of the day with Jim. They took a walk, he said, and Jim was attacked with a fit of hiccuping that continued for nearly an hour. Ronay said Jim didn't look well and he told him so. Jim rarely complained and shrugged it off, saying he felt fine. But Ronay said that at the end of the walk, Jim had difficulty breathing when they carried firewood up to the apartment from the building's courtyard. Before leaving, Ronay recommended that they attend a screening that night of *Pursued*, an offbeat American western starring Robert Mitchum. Pam the next day told police they had seen a film called *Death Valley*.

What happened following the movie was, for a long time, open to conjecture – the subject of wild disagreement and controversy.

I was living in London in 1972, the following year, and I visited Paris several times in my search for information. The stories I was told about Jim's death were confusing. The one I heard most often was that Jim died from an overdose of heroin in a nightclub called the Rock'n'Roll Circus. This is a version I heard repeatedly during my interviews and later was confirmed by sources in the junkie underground talking to Hervé Muller, a French journalist who picked up some of the threads of the story after I returned to the U.S.

Junkies are generally not known for their reliability. Usually they are anxious to say anything they think the listener wants to hear, in exchange, they hope, for enough money to score another bag of relief. None of the sources with whom Hervé talked was paid for information beyond the cost of coffee at some sidewalk cafe. Nor was any 'ulterior' motive apparent, at least to Hervé or me. Junkies generally don't look for publicity and there is little status to be gained amongst other junkies, or anyone else, to say you shared heroin with Jim Morrison the night he died of an overdose.

Of course, there's always a chance that some nut made up the whole story and that it started going around, building up, becoming more elaborate as it travelled. But the lack of contradiction on the basic points of the story is impressive.

Nor does it seem that this version of Jim's death was a fabrication created to counter the 'official' version. To the contrary, the 'official' version – death by a heart attack in a bathtub – seemed totally unknown in the junkie underground until its members were interviewed.

Jim was familiar with the junkie underground, or at least aware of it, not because of Pamela's sporadic use of the drug, but because of the dives in which he chose to drink. The most notable of these in Paris at the time was the Circus, where the walls were covered with huge photographs of rock stars wearing clown costumes. Earlier, this was the slickest rock club in Paris – where Led Zeppelin, Richie Havens, and Johnny Winter had played – but by Summer 1971, it had slid close to the bottom. Rock and roll was still the music played, but now most of the action wasn't on the dance floor, it was in the toilets. Occasionally the place was raided by police and that would precipitate an exodus that related to the junkies' version of Jim's death.

The Circus was situated at 57 rue de Seine, on the Left Bank near the river, and it backed up to a much more respectable club, called the Alcazar. The Alcazar, at 62 rue Mazarine, presented an expensive dinner-spectacle of French music and scantily clad dancers, catering to a crowd of middle-aged French businessmen. The club was large, seating close to a thousand patrons on three levels, surrounding a stage about four times the size of that of the more famous Latin Quarter. For some of the junkies in the Circus, when police arrived, the escape route was through the Circus kitchen, which had a back door leading into the Alcazar's kitchen. It was a simple matter then to slip from the kitchen through the darkened club and onto the adjoining street without being noticed.

According to information gathered by Hervé Muller, one of the dealers on the scene in the summer of 1971 was a Chinese called 'Le Chinoise'. Supposedly, he had a laboratory for making heroin in Marseille, which explains why he happened to

Jim 'in hiding' in a Paris cafe. He left America
full of plans for a new beginning.

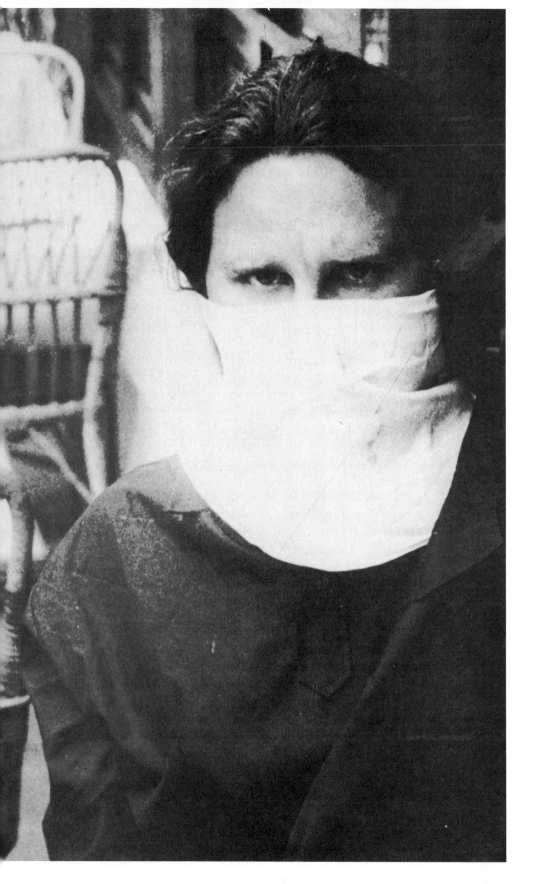

have such unusually potent heroin to sell, running to about 30 per cent 'pure' instead of the customary 5 to 10 per cent. The way the story goes, 'Le Chinoise', who was not known to use heroin himself, sold a quantity to a second-level dealer named Michel, who in turn sold a smaller quantity to someone called 'Le Petit Bernard', charging him $100. Bernard then sold that packet to Jim for about $200, warning him of the potency.

'That's okay,' Jim reportedly said, 'I'm used to it.' All sources say Jim seemed to be nervous, upset.

All sources also told Hervé Muller that the final transaction took place in the men's room of the Circus, where Jim snorted the heroin, then slumped into a comatose state. The junkies present heaved him to his feet between them, guiding him back into the night club, then through the adjoining kitchens to the Alcazar, and into a cab on the street.

At this point, it is generally agreed that Jim was still alive. This is reasonable. In most heroin overdoses, the victim generally dies after one or two hours of lethargy, stupor, and coma. The way this story ends, Jim was returned to his flat and dumped into a bathtub full of cold water in an attempt to revive him, standard treatment for an overdose, although there is some question about its practicality. That was one version of how Jim died. Of course it wasn't the only one.

In a second, far more innocent story, outlined in a statement given to Paris police the day Jim died, and thereafter described as The Official Version of the Death, Pam said that she and Jim returned to the flat from the movie theatre about 1am and after she washed some dishes and Jim watched some home movies projected on the apartment wall, they went to bed, falling asleep about 2.30am while listening to some records.

About an hour later, Pam told police (in a deposition taken several hours after Jim died), she was awakened by Jim's noisy breathing. She said she wasn't sure of the time, because there was no clock in the bedroom. She thought Jim might be suffocating and shook him. He didn't wake up. She slapped him a few times and then shook him again. Finally, he opened his eyes. He told Pam that he wasn't feeling well and after pacing in the bedroom for a minute or two, told Pam that he wanted to take a warm bath.

Once in the tub, Pam told police, Jim said he felt nauseous. Pam brought an orange cooking pot from the kitchen and Jim vomited. Pam cleaned the pot in the nearby sink and Jim threw up a second time, expelling a quantity of blood. Again Pam cleaned the pot and a third time Jim vomited, now a few blood clots. She told police that Jim insisted 'it's over'; he was feeling better and he didn't want her to call a doctor. Pam quoted Jim as saying he would finish his bath and he urged Pam to return to bed. She said colour had returned to his face and she felt 'reassured', so she did as he suggested, falling asleep.

Pam said she 'awoke with a start' some time later and saw that she was in bed alone. She got up and went to the bathroom, where she found Jim still in the bath. His eyes were closed and he was smiling, she said, his head tilted back on the edge of the tub, turned to one side. Pam said she thought he was joking and, according to Diane Gardiner, she stood there talking to him for some time. She told him it was a dumb joke. She said she knew what he was doing; he was trying to scare her. Slowly, Pam did become scared. She noticed there was some blood under one nostril. She shook him.

She told police she thought she could awaken him. She tried to get him out of the tub and couldn't. That was when, panicked because she couldn't speak French and telephone for help, she called Alain Ronay at Agnes Varda's house. Years later, Varda said that the call came about 8am, an hour at which she never answered the telephone. But Ronay picked up the receiver and heard Pam say, 'I can't wake him up. I think he's dying.' Ronay went to Varda's room, woke her, and she called for an ambulance immediately. Ronay wrote out the Morrison address as Varda dialled the emergency number for the fire brigade. Ronay hurriedly told her not to reveal Jim's celebrity and when the telephone conversation was completed, they drove to the Morrison apartment.

In interviews she and Ronay gave to *Paris Match* in 1991, both he and Varda say that when they arrived, they saw firemen on the street. Ronay asked, 'Is he okay?' and was told to ask his questions upstairs. Ronay and Varda went up to the second floor appartment.

*Jim and Pam in Paris shortly before Jim's
untimely death in July, 1971.*

There is a contradiction in the Ronay and Varda stories at this point. Varda remembers clearly that when they arrived, Jim was still in the tub, surrounded by members of the fire brigade. On the other hand, Ronay says that Jim was already on the bed and that he never saw the body. Varda's accurate description of the death scene in the bathroom gives credence to her story over Ronay's.

Fire Lt. Alain Raisson said in his statement to police that he and his men responded to a call of 'asphyxie', or asphyxiation, and were greeted by a 'young woman who could not speak French'. This was Pamela, who led them to the bathroom where they found 'a man in the bath, completely naked and heavily built. His head was above the water, reclining to one side on the edge of the bath. The bath was full of water, pinkish in colour, and his right arm was resting on the side of the bath.' Both the water and the body were described as 'lukewarm'.

With his men, Raisson removed the body from the tub and carried it into the bedroom, where they placed it on the floor and attempted cardio-pulmonary resuscitation. Raisson said a quantity of blood ran from Jim's right nostril when they laid him down. When it was clear that Jim was dead, Raisson had his men move the body to the bed.

A second report was filed the same day by Jacques Manchez, a police officer who arrived to find Jim covered by a spread on the bed. He noted blood running from one nostril, a clot closing the other one, and ordered the spread pulled back. He then searched for any signs of 'trauma', such as wounds or needle marks, and found none. He also reported that there were no signs of 'disorder' in the room (evidence of a fight).

When Ronay and Varda entered the apartment they went directly to Pam, who was wearing a white robe she had bought in Algiers. She merely said Jim was dead. Before they could talk further, the police arrived, with Jacques Manchez in charge. In an effort to cloak the death in further mystery, Ronay and Pam told the officer that Jim's name was Douglas James Morrison, transposing the first and middle names. They also identified Jim merely as a poet. Manchez was suspicious, asking, 'How could Jim be a poet? He was so young.'

Ronay said, 'Was Victor Hugo born with a white beard? Did Rimbaud have one when he died?'

Manchez asked how a mere poet could have afforded such a spacious apartment in such a good neighbourhood.

Ronay said Jim was independently wealthy.

Their conversation was interrupted by the arrival of Dr. Max Vassille, a physician on the staff of the Paris Medical University. He was called by the office of Police Superintendent Robert Berry in accordance with the penal procedures code. Manchez told Ronay that the doctor's findings would determine whether or not the police would open an investigation into the death.

Ronay asked what sort of investigation he was talking about. Manchez said that if the doctor found anything out of order, many officers would be involved.

When Dr. Vassille emerged from the bedroom, he asked Pam if Jim used drugs. Ronay answered for her. He said Jim drank, but never used drugs; he never even smoked marijuana in Los Angeles, where it was as freely available as cigarettes.

The doctor's official statement filed later that day ruled that death was due to natural causes. He noted the blood around the nostrils, but said there were no signs of trauma (wounds, puncture marks). Vassille also referred to a conversation he apparently had with Ronay, who said Jim had experienced chest pains for a period of time. The doctor conjectured that there were coronary problems, aggravated by 'abusive drinking'. The change in temperature represented by the warm bath then pushed Jim over the edge, resulting in 'myocardial infarction' – a heart attack.

While the doctor made his examination, the telephone rang. It was Pamela's friend, the Count. Pam took the phone into another room and told her friend that Jim was dead. The Count was with the British pop star Marianne Faithfull at the time of the call, a fact that, later, would explain how the story of Jim's death began to leak out. Apparently, Pam never told anyone what she and the Count said and the Count died a few years later of a heroin overdose.

After hanging up the phone, Pam returned to Ronay and

Varda, taking Ronay's arm. Ronay said, 'Tell me, quickly, how he died.' Pam told him. Ronay and Varda agreed that they had to keep it quiet.

At 3.40 that afternoon, Ronay and Pam went to police head-quarters and gave their depositions, required before the case could be closed. Pam went first – with Ronay translating for her – telling Officer Manchez that shortly after she and Jim had come to Paris, while living in the Hotel de Nice, before moving into the apartment, Jim had a breathing problem, accompanied by a chronic cough. She called a doctor, who came to the hotel and prescribed a medicine normally used by asthmatics. Pam said she couldn't remember the doctor's name and the medicine was thrown away. She added that Jim didn't like doctors and never took care of himself.

In his statement, Ronay gave the police more testimony regarding Jim's poor health. He said, 'I'm sure that my friend didn't take any drugs. He often talked about the stupidity of young people taking drugs. He thought this problem was extremely serious.' He then told the story of his walk with Jim the previous day, when Jim had had an 'attack of hiccups' and had trouble carrying firewood from the courtyard to the flat.

The following day, Police Superintendent Robert Berry filed the last official report, summarizing the statements of the fire brigade, the local police precinct, Dr. Vassille, Pamela, and Ronay. This was a formality required in the filing of a burial certificate, part of closing the case.

'Nothing suspicious was noticed on the spot either in the apartment or on the body, which bore no trace of blows, lesions, or needle marks,' Berry wrote. With no signs of 'foul play', no autopsy was required and Pam was given permission to proceed with the funeral arrangements.

Before I tell what I believe really happened, let me explain why *No One Here Gets Out Alive* ended so ambiguously, hinting strongly that Jim might have engineered a hoax and was still alive. At the time I wrote the book, I really wasn't sure how Jim died, although I was satisfied that he was dead. When Hervé Muller presented the Rock'n'Roll Circus scenario, somehow I doubted it. (Although, to this day, Hervé stands by the story.) It just didn't feel right and of all the variations in Pam's story which emerged once she was back in the United States and confiding in friends, none ever mentioned the Circus or this band of mysterious junkies.

While writing *No One Here*, I was also picking up other theories, right, left, and sideways. Jim had been stabbed to death, or killed by someone sticking pins in a voodoo doll. One story had his death part of a serpentine conspiracy connecting the deaths of John Kennedy, Robert Kennedy, Martin Luther King, Jimi Hendrix, Janis Joplin, the Kent State Five, and several Black Panthers. Each was more ridiculous than the last.

I had to finish the book. I didn't believe the official story for a minute and I didn't feel comfortable with Hervé Muller's carefully researched nightclub toilet overdose. So I reported the many scenarios, a long list that included the possibility that Jim wasn't dead at all, but merely living out an elaborately conceived and brilliantly executed hoax. I believed that this was something that, with Pamela's help, Jim could have pulled off.

Certainly it was something he could have conceived. In college he had explored, intellectually, the possibility that Jesus Christ's death was a hoax. Jim also had joked about faking his own death even before the band had its first hit record. In his interview with me for *Rolling Stone*, Jim talked about the possibility that at some time in the future he could appear with a different identity, wearing a suit and tie. With a Hollywood screenwriter he had devised a plot about someone who disappeared into the jungle in search of 'absolute zero'.

I decided to write two last chapters, one of which had Jim dying of an overdose, the other having him disappear into North Africa, much like his hero, the poet Arthur Rimbaud. I suggested to the publisher that if, say, 10,000 copies of the book were published, 5,000 should end with an overdose caused by the combination of alcohol and heroin, the other 5,000 with the hoax. I asked that the books then be distributed randomly and without comment; let the readers discover the

Jim in a Paris cafe. He shaved off his beard, lost
weight, but the dream soon faded.

different endings on their own. I still think it was a good idea, but the publisher disagreed, so *No One Here Gets Out Alive* ended ambiguously, with both final chapters blended into one, leaving the reader uncertain. Of course this served the original purpose, fanning the flames of the rumour that Jim was not dead, but alive somewhere.

The years passed and while I remained convinced that Jim was dead, I still didn't know what happened. At the same time, I came to believe that I might have neglected, or at least underestimated and misunderstood, Pamela's role in Jim's life, and I began to consider writing a second, smaller book, or perhaps a screenplay, focusing on their romance.

I re-interviewed some of my earlier subjects, among them Diane Gardiner. After Jim was buried and when Pam returned to the U.S., Pam moved into Diane's cottage in Sausalito, California. Diane, who was then working as a publicist for the Jefferson Airplane, had been one of Pam's closest confidantes in Los Angeles and I figured that if anyone knew what happened, or at least knew what Pam said happened, it was Diane.

Diane apologized for not telling me more in interviews she gave me when I was researching *No One Here Gets Out Alive*. She said she promised Pamela not to reveal anything about Jim's death and at the time, Pam was still alive, so Diane said she felt bound to her pledge. Now – ten years after Jim's death – Diane told me that when Pam returned from Europe 'she was a real case, just devastated'. Diane said that for several months Pam walked around talking to herself, rambling and making no sense, and when she did make sense, she blamed herself for Jim's death.

'I've never seen anyone feeling so guilty,' Diane told me. 'She had tried to devote her whole life to one person. That was it. That was her life. Her whole life was him. And to have that kicked out from under you...'

As Diane and Pam spent more time together, fragments of the story came together, forming a believable scenario, explaining the source of Pam's guilt.

Apparently Jim and Pam had stopped at one or more side-

walk cafes on the way home from the movie, where Jim consumed several drinks. (This explains the arrival home at 1am,
quite late for returning from a movie theatre.) At home, Jim
mixed another drink as Pam lined up some white powder on
a table top.

At this point, Diane is a bit vague. Jim had known about
Pam's heroin use, but most agree that apparently he didn't
know how frequently she used it. Diane told me that Pam
seemed able to use it on a daily basis for a while, then merely
stop, suffering rarely from withdrawal. And, Diane said, to
her knowledge, Pam never used heroin with Jim or in his presence, at least until now. Jim disapproved of heroin. This was
confirmed by everyone I talked to. Danny Sugerman, the 14-
year-old high school student who hung out at the Doors'
office and ten years later helped me get *No One Here Gets Out
Alive* published, said Jim actually lectured him about 'the evils
and horrors of heroin'.

So, Diane told me, when Jim saw Pam bent over a line of
white powder, it is possible he thought it was cocaine. Jim
liked cocaine. There is no reason to think he would have done
anything but smile and join Pam on the couch and inhale the
next line of powder.

On the other hand, he could also have sensed, or realized,
that it was heroin. Diane told me that, according to Pam, the
talk about Jim's depression was real. The past year or so,
many projects had been started or discussed – a screenplay
with Michael McClure, a poetry album with John Haeny, a
stage show with Fred Myrow, a book about the Miami trial, an
opera, on and on. None had been completed. Most were still-
born. In addition, Jim was overweight, alcoholic, and impo-
tent (a side-effect of his alcoholism).

The constant drinking only aggravated the depression. Jim
had written a few lines in one of his notebooks that said,
'Leave the informed sense in our wake/you be the Christ on
this package tour/Money beats soul/Last words, last words,

*Overleaf: Left The French doctor's report giving
heart attack as cause of death. Right: The US
Embassy death report.*

RAPPORT MÉDICO-LÉGAL

Je soussigné **Max VASSILLE ,médecçin assermenté**
Docteur en Médecine de la Faculté de **PARIS**
demeurant à **Paris 3I rue du ᴿenard**
requis par Monsieur **BERRY Robert**   Commissaire de Police
de **l'ARSENAL**
Officier de Police Judiciaire,
agissant sur délégation de Monsieur le Procureur. de la · République
conformément à l'article 74 du Code de Procédure Pénale, serment préa-
lablement prêté de donner mon avis en mon· honneur et conscience,
me suis présente·le **3 Juillet I97I**   à   **I8**   h
ʟ (1)   **I7 rue Beautreillis escalier A 3e étage droite**
afin d'examiner le corps identifié par l'enquête judiciaire comme étant
celui d **u** nommé **MORRISSON James**
âgé   de **28** ans.

J'ai constaté : que le corps ne présente en dehors de
lividités cadavériques habituelles aucune trace su
pecte de traumatisme ou de lésion quelconque.Un. p
de sand au niveau des narines.L'evolution d'un éta
de santé de Mr MORRISON telle qu'elle nous a été
raconté par un ami présent sur les lieux peut se
reconstituer ainsi,Mr MORRISON se plaignait depuis
quelques semaines de douleurs précordiales avec
dyspnée d'effort il s'agit manifestement de troubl
coronariens peut être aggravés par l'abus de boiss
alcoolisées.On peut concevoir qu'à l'occasion d'un
changement de température extérieure suivie d'un b
ces troubles se soient aggravés brusquement donnan
le classique infarctus du myocarde cause de mort
subite.Deson examen je conclus.

que la mort a été provoquée par un arrêt
cardiaque (mort naturelle).

Paris, le **3 Juillet I97I**

(1) Lieu de l'examen

SELECTIVE SERVICE ADMINISTRATION

REPORT OF THE DEATH OF AN AMERICAN CITIZEN

FINAL   American Embassy, Paris, France, August 11, 1971
                              (Place and date)

Name in full __James Douglas MORRISON__   Occupation __Singer__

Native or naturalized __BORN ON December 8, 1943 AT Clearwater,__ Last known address
                                                    Florida
in the United States __8216 Norton Avenue, Los Angeles, California__

Date of death __July__   __3__   __5:00 a.m.__   __1971__   Age __27 years__
              (Month)   (Day)   (Hour)   (Minute)   (Year)   (As nearly as can be ascertained)

Place of death __17, rue Beautreillis, Paris 4, France__
              (Number and street) or (Hospital or hotel)   (City)   (Country)

Cause of death __Heart Failure__
                              (Include authority for statement)

As certified by Dr. Max Vassille, 31, rue du Renard, Paris, France

Disposition of the remains __Interred in Pere Lachaise Cemetery, 16th Division, Paris,__
France on July 7, 1971.

Local law as to disinterring remains __May be disinterred at any time upon the request of__
nearest relative or legal representative of the estate. See Decree Law of December
31, 1941, Journal Officiel, January 26-27, 1942, Page 378.

Disposition of the effects __In the custody of Pamela Courson, friend.__

Person or official responsible for custody of effects and accounting therefor __Rear Admiral George S.__
Informed by telegram: Morrison, father.

NAME	ADDRESS	RELATIONSHIP	DATE SENT
N/A			

Copy of this report sent to:

NAME	ADDRESS	RELATIONSHIP	DATE SENT
ear Admiral George S. Morrison	Chief Naval Operations	Father	August 11, 1971
	OPO 3B - Room 4E 552		
	Pentagon, Washington, D.C. 20350		

Traveling or residing abroad with relatives or friends as follows:

NAME	ADDRESS	RELATIONSHIP
Miss Pamela Courson	17, rue Beautreillis	Friend
	75 - Paris 4, France	

Other known relatives (not given above):

NAME	ADDRESS	RELATIONSHIP
Unknown		

This information and data concerning an inventory of the effects, accounts, etc., have been placed
under File 234 in the correspondence of this office.

Remarks: __U.S. passport number J 900083, issued at Los Angeles, California,__
on August 7, 1968 cancelled and returned to father.

Filing date and place of French Death Certificate: July 3, 1971 at the Town Hall
of Paris 4, France.
                                              (Continue on reverse if necessary.)

                              Mary Ann Meysenburg
                              Mary Ann Meysenburg
[SEAL]   (Signature on all copies)
No fee prescribed.   Vice Consul_____ of the United States of America

Over

out.' Later, two of Jim's biographers would use these lines to support a theory that his death was likely a suicide.

Diane doesn't dismiss that theory, at least not entirely. She told me that when Jim saw the powder lined up so neatly on the table top, he may have known it wasn't cocaine, but heroin, and knew what dangers lay in its use, especially in combination with alcohol. (When two central nervous system depressants, in this case alcohol and heroin, come together synergistically, they create a knockout punch: one plus one equals six!)

Danny Sugerman told me a slightly different version of the same story. I now know that when Danny edited *No One Here Gets Out Alive* in the late 1970s, he knew that Jim had died of an overdose, but he never told me. But later Danny told me that he and Pamela had shared both heroin and sex after Pam left Diane Gardiner's home and returned to Los Angeles. Danny said that when Pam talked about Jim's death to Danny, she also pledged him not to tell 'Hopkins', who then was trying to interview her. Danny was the one who merged the book's two last chapters into one, which gave him an opportunity to tell the truth. But he remained loyal to Pamela rather than tell what he knew, even though Pam was dead.

I re-interviewed Danny about the same time I talked to Diane Gardiner, in 1981. *No One Here Gets Out Alive* was, by then, a huge success and Jim had been dead for more than ten years, so Danny talked more candidly. (Although he has never yet admitted to me that he had withheld the true story of Jim's death while working on the manuscript.) In our recorded conversation, he told me he had asked Pam about Paris and heroin. At first she told him that Jim would never use heroin. At the time of this conversation, Danny said, both he and Pam were stoned on heroin. 'If he were alive today,' she said, 'he'd kill both of us, Danny.'

Danny told me, 'That didn't answer my question. You couldn't confront Pam on this,' he said. 'It was the most painful moment of her life.'

I asked Danny, 'She never said anything about heroin being a part of his death?'

Danny said, 'I seem to remember her saying something. In

*Singer Patti Smith is just one of thousands who
have paid homage to Morrison at his grave.*

a real stupor, when you're nodding out, you don't know who you're talking to, you don't even know if you're talking, and I feel not unqualified to tell this story, but I feel not awfully secure in its reportage, because I was awful high, too. But I do remember a conversation regarding her guilt and her getting really down on herself...something to the effect: she was busted, Jim found it [the heroin].

'What's this!' Jim said. (As Danny recalled the conversation.)

'It's coke!'

Jim dumped a quantity on the table, deftly pushing it into long, thick lines, probably with the edge of a paper matchbook or a credit card. He inhaled the first line.

Pam said, 'Jim, don't do too much. Jim, don't do too much!'

Danny again: '...rather than say, "Jim, it's smack." Because she had been hiding it from him, and she knew damned well he did not do that. And he did not want her to do it. He saw what heroin did to friends like Tim Hardin. [Another singer-songwriter who died of a heroin overdose.] He knew the hazards of it.

'So I remember a guilt feeling, and an implication...that Jim had discovered her stash and Pam said, "Oh, Jim, it's just coke," which he really wasn't into, at that point anyway, and Jim said, "Let's do some." He put it out and snorted it like it was coke.'

Danny insisted that he didn't know the true story, because this was only one of many that Pamela told, and the one she told most consistently was the 'official' version, of a heart attack in the bathtub. It is, however, the story he believes.

It is the story that was told by Alain Ronay and Agnes Varda to *Paris Match* in 1991, twenty years after Jim's death, that makes this story most real.

Pam took Ronay's arm in the Paris apartment as the doctor was examining Jim's body. Pam said she and Jim had been snorting heroin for two days. Pam said they snorted heroin the night before and again that afternoon, after Jim had taken his walk with Ronay and before he went out to dinner alone. When they returned home from the movie and the bistro, the heroin came out again. In this version, Pam did not mention washing dishes, or say Jim watched home movies. Now Pam said Jim started playing the Doors' recordings, including the first album, which contained the song, 'The End'. She said Jim got out of bed and snorted some more heroin, so, she added, Jim actually had consumed more than she did. She said that one of the Doors' records was playing when they nodded off to sleep.

Ronay quoted Varda as asking, 'Who had the heroin? Was it you?'

Pamela said, 'Of course...'

Pam said she woke up to Jim's heavy breathing. This matched the story she told police. She said that when Jim failed to awake when she shook him, she screamed, and began slapping him 'very, very hard'. Finally, he opened his eyes, but he didn't seem to know where he was. She said she helped him to walk to the bathroom and assisted him into the tub.

Agnes asked her who had run the water in the tub. Pam said she couldn't remember.

Pam told Ronay she returned to the bedroom, fell asleep, waking some time later. When she found Jim missing from their bed, she went to the bathroom and saw him in the tub with blood running from his nose. He started vomiting, she said, so she ran to the kitchen, returning with an orange cooking pot. Three times Jim vomited and each time Pam said she cleaned the pot, returning to bed once more when assured by Jim that he was feeling better.

Varda patted Pam's hand and told her that Jim died at least an hour and a half before the firemen arrived; there was nothing she could do.

Pam said, 'Jim looked so calm. He smiled.' She was in shock.

Varda continued to reassure Pam.

Pam suddenly produced a piece of paper that she said was a marriage application she and Jim had taken out in 1967 in Colorado, but never acted on. She asked her friends if they thought the Paris police would accept it as proof that she and Jim were married.

As the day brightened, the fiction grew. Alan Ronay said he didn't want Jim's death and burial to become the circus that

Last Will and Testament

of

JAMES D. MORRISON

573952

BK 1979 PG 0430

I, JAMES D. MORRISON, being of sound and disposing mind, memory and understanding, and after consideration for all persons, the objects of my bounty, and with full knowledge of the nature and extent of my assets, do hereby make, publish and declare this my Last Will and Testament, as follows:

FIRST: I declare that I am a resident of Los Angeles County, California; that I am unmarried and have no children.

SECOND: I direct the payment of all debts and expenses of last illness.

THIRD: I do hereby devise and bequeath each and every thing of value of which I may die possessed, including real property, personal property and mixed properties to PAMELA S. COURSON of Los Angeles County.

In the event the said PAMELA S. COURSON should predecease me, or fail to survive for a period of three months following the date of my death, then and in such event, the devise and bequest to her shall fail and the same is devised and bequeathed instead to my brother, ANDREW MORRISON of Monterey, California, and to my sister, ANNE R. MORRISON of Coronado Beach, California, to share and share alike; provided, however, further that in the event either of them should predecease me, then and in such event, the devise and bequest shall go to the other.

FOURTH: I do hereby appoint PAMELA S. COURSON and MAX FINK, jointly, Executors, or Executor and Executrix, as the case may be, of my estate, giving to said persons, and each of them, full power of appointment of substitution in their place and stead by their Last Will and Testament, or otherwise.

In the event said PAMELA S. COURSON shall survive me and be living at the time of her appointment, then in such event, bond is hereby waived.

I subscribe my name to this Will this _12_ day of February, 1969, at Beverly Hills, California.

ADMITTED TO PROBATE

AUG 17 1971

JAMES D. MORRISON

Attest: William G. Sharp, County Clerk
_____ Deputy

had attended the recent deaths of Jimi Hendrix and Janis Joplin. As Pam and Ronay and Varda – and soon, Robin Wertle – devised a plan for handling Jim's burial, the 'official' version of the death took its final form.

Part of the cover-up was to avoid mentioning anything if anyone telephoned. The first call – forgetting the one from the Count – was from a male friend of the woman from whom Jim and Pam leased the flat. He had seen Pam a few times before Jim joined her in Paris and he wondered if she was free that night to go out with him. She said no, she was going to stay with Jim. The next time the phone rang, Ronay took it. It was Hervé Muller, who hadn't seen Jim in three weeks and was calling to say hello, maybe make some plans. Ronay told Muller that Jim and Pam were away for the weekend.

By now, the news of Jim's death was travelling along the Paris underground and that night (Saturday) about midnight it reached the ears of Cameron Watson, an American expatriate who was then working as a disc jockey in a discotheque called Le Bulle. Two drug-dealers entered Watson's glass-enclosed booth.

'Hey,' said one, 'I just scored three-thousand francs of "H" for Marianne Faithfull and she was crying. She said Jim Morrison is dead.'

Watson knew that Marianne was an addict and that she had been in Paris that week. He did not know that Pam's friend the Count was with Faithfull when the Count called Pam, but Watson believed what Faithfull told him. He stopped the music and said, 'Jim Morrison was found dead this morning.' He made the announcement first in English, then in French.

Jean-Bernard Hebey, who had a radio show on Radio Luxembourg, was at Le Bulle and he took the story to work with him, announcing the death on his show on Sunday. The story now had a large audience and by Monday morning the national newspapers in England were calling the London office of Elektra Records for confirmation.

Clive Selwood, who ran the office, called Elektra's Paris office. The Paris office didn't even know Jim was living in the French capital. Clive then called the American Embassy and the Paris police. Both agencies had no knowledge of the death.

Clive decided to call Bill Siddons in Los Angeles. With the nine-hour time difference, he woke the manager. 'Bill,' he said, 'I can't substantiate it in any way, but we're getting reports that Jim is dead.'

Siddons almost laughed. 'Oh, come on, Clive...' For years, Siddons had heard similar rumours. Jim had died of an overdose or an automobile accident or a fall from a hotel balcony. Clive said he had taken calls from several journalists whom he respected, so Siddons dialled Jim and Pam's Paris number. But there was no answer and he returned to his bed. Awaking several hours later, Siddons tried again and Pam answered. Initially, she denied that Jim was dead, but finally admitted the truth. Pam didn't like the Doors' manager any more than she liked the other Doors, but she knew that he'd take care of business and be able to bring some needed cash. Billy caught the earliest flight to assist with final arrangements and to help Pam pack for a return to California.

At about the same time, Jim's lawyer Max Fink said he received a collect call from Pam. He described her condition as incoherent, greatly agitated. Fink told her to hire a Los Angeles-based private detective named John O'Grady (who had known Jim slightly) and to fly him to Paris immediately to handle everything discreetly. Fink says Pam hung up abruptly, calling back later to explain – calmly now – that everything was under control.

Through the entire weekend, Jim's body had remained on the double bed in the master bedroom, packed in ice, according to Pam's wishes. On Monday, with Ronay's assistance, a mortuary was contracted and a varnished oak coffin was delivered to the apartment. The body was placed inside.

Siddons arrived Tuesday morning and agreed with Pam that the death should be kept quiet. That day and the next, Tuesday and Wednesday, Siddons helped make final arrangements and assisted Pam pack her and Jim's belongings, while Ronay went to Père-Lachaise Cemetery and purchased a plot. This was one of Paris's most famous cemeteries and, according to Pam, Jim had visited it and expressed a desire to be buried there, so he could share a final resting place with Chopin, Bizet, Edith Piaf, Oscar Wilde, Balzac, and Molière.

Ronay handled the purchase of the plot, turning down a location close to Oscar Wilde's tomb, taking a less propitious spot. Siddons and Wertle then visited the funeral home to make final arrangements, requesting a hearse and four pallbearers.

(Danny Sugerman told me that while helping Pam pack, Siddons found heroin in the apartment, but Danny also quoted Pam as saying that regarding Jim's death, Siddons knew only what he was told. In all my conversations with Siddons, he confirmed this. Apparently, he was told nothing about the role heroin played in Jim's death.)

On Wednesday morning, the day before the burial, Pamela filed the death certificate with the American Embassy, identifying Jim only as 'James Douglas Morrison, poet.' Nothing was said about his true celebrity.

The next day, Thursday, Jim's body was lowered into a grave on a tiny plot between two large marble sepulchres at Père-Lachaise. There were only five mourners present: Pam, Bill Siddons, Alain Ronay, Agnes Varda, and Robin Wertle.

In the years that followed, Pam fought for acceptance as Jim's heir and wife. Initially, it seemed quite simple. Jim had had his lawyer, Max Fink, draft a simple, two-page will in 1969, naming Pamela S. Courson as his sole heir and, with Fink, his co-executor. (In the event that Pam died first, Jim's estate was to be shared equally by his brother and sister.)

In November 1971, four months after Jim died, in an effort to bolster her claim, and to be granted an allowance and an advance from the estate – which was then still in probate – Pam filed a 'declaration in support of widow's allowance', claiming 'at all times since September 30, 1967, I have considered that I was married to James D. Morrison, and that I was in fact his wife at the time of his death and am now his widow'. It was in 1967, as 'Light My Fire' was finally dropping off the charts, that Pam said she and Jim spent a night in Colorado Springs. Earlier, she had Jim ask Max Fink which states had the loosest laws recognizing common law marriage.

In her court statement, Pam said, 'Jim reported to me that he learned from an attorney that to create a marriage in the state of Colorado it was sufficient if two people stayed together, had marital relations and agreed to thereby be husband and wife, if in fact they thereafter conducted and held themselves out as each other's spouse. We spent the night at a hotel, had sexual relations and agreed that we would forever after be husband and wife. We very briefly honeymooned in Colorado and then continued our [the Doors] tour.'

Pam's statement went on to say that during their relationship, all her living expenses were paid from Jim's earnings. All credit card charges were paid, she said, her medical, dental, clothing, and entertainment expenses were paid, and she and Jim were given $2,500 in cash each month for incidentals. Now, she said, she was penniless.

In December 1971, the three surviving Doors filed papers of their own in court, making claims against the Morrison estate, most of it for a loan they said Jim had taken to help pay some of his legal costs. Although the sum asked, less than $36,000, was small, considering the size of the estate, it was sufficient to bottle things up in court for two years. Then in April 1974, the Doors came back with another lawsuit, now requesting repayment of a $250,000 loan allegedly made by the Doors Corporation to Jim as an advance against his share of future royalties. At the same time, Max Fink, who continued to represent the other Doors, submitted a bill for approximately $75,000 for work done on the Phoenix and Miami trials. Next the Miami law firm filed suit for unpaid services.

Eventually, a compromise was reached. Pam relented, agreeing to pay everyone. Max Fink said he authorized a loan to Pam in the interim, much of which was spent on a mink coat and a yellow Volkswagen Beetle. Then, as the final accounting of the estate was being made, Pam died. If she had lived, she would have received about $500,000 right away, plus a quarter of everything the Doors would make in the future, a sum that subsequently proved to be worth millions.

What really happened in Paris on July 3, 1971?

I am certain that Jim died of an overdose of heroin, complicated by the alcohol level in his bloodstream. What generally happens when these two 'drugs' come together and deliver their synergistic hammer-blow, is described as a 'massive pul-

Morrison's grave in Père-Lachaise cemetery,
Paris, surrounded by gifts and plaques from fans.

monary edema', a kind of mega heart attack, where the victim, poisoned by the combination, slumps, froth spilling from his mouth and nostrils.

Of course, no one will ever know. The only person present at the time of Jim's death was Pamela, who may not even have known herself what happened, and if she did, she took the full story to her grave. Obviously, she had something to do with Jim's death, may even have unwittingly caused it, at least in her own mind, by having the heroin in the apartment and sharing it with him.

I thought it was interesting that before signing over the rights to their daughter's life to Oliver Stone for his movie *The Doors*, her parents had it written into the contract that the script make no connection whatsoever between Pamela and Jim's death. In other words, if Stone was going to portray Jim's death in any way, he was to stick to the 'official' version. (Which he did.) Did Pam's parents know what happened, and share their daughter's grief and guilt? Had they become partners in the conspiracy to cover up the true cause of Jim's death?

When I was researching *No One Here Gets Out Alive*, I met Pam once, over lunch. I left the restaurant feeling I had just spent a couple of hours with the most beautiful, fragile, vulnerable, and manipulative woman I had ever met, but I had learned very little about Jim, or her, or their relationship. And I was told nothing about Jim's death.

I asked her why she had agreed to meet me. She said Jim had liked me, and I had written positive stories about him and the Doors. She also wanted to know why I was writing the book. I told her that I was more affected by Jim's death than I thought our relationship warranted and I wanted to find out why. She said nothing, merely nodded.

At the time of the meeting, two years after Jim's death, I had no idea what Pam was doing for a living. She avoided answering such questions by saying only that she was trying to keep Jim's memory alive and untarnished. For example, she told me she had won a fight to keep 'Light My Fire' from being sold for a television commercial. All her other comments were superficial and unrevealing. She seemed nervous, but in control of the situation, as if she were caught in a scene she wanted to end, and was handling it, nonetheless.

Years later, Danny Sugerman, and others, told me her life was a mess. Danny said he had spent a lot of time with her, frequently shared his own heroin with her, sometimes gave her part of the $75 a week that he was getting from Ray Manzarek (as Manzarek's publicist). Danny said he thought Pam was seriously disturbed, said she sometimes sat near the telephone, waiting for Jim to call. Danny quoted her as saying, 'My old man hasn't called! He promised me he'd call!'

Implying that Jim was alive, all evidence – and her own tortured stories – to the contrary.

When Pam died, on 25 April 1974, at age 27 – Jim's age when he died – she was working as a prostitute, something she often said that Jim had predicted was her destiny. A man who had worked as Jim's occasional limousine driver was her live-in boyfriend and it was clear, from the autopsy, that an overdose of heroin was the cause of death.

Pam once had asked Max Fink to draw up her will, but he refused, so she died intestate, which meant her quarter-share of all future Doors earnings went to her next-of-kin, her parents, Columbus (Corky) Courson, and his wife Pearl (Penny). Almost immediately, Jim's parents, Admiral George Morrison and his wife Clara, entered the fray, demanding their 'fair share' as stated in the California probate code. On 10 January 1975, the two sets of parents signed an agreement dividing equally the proceeds from Jim's quarter-share of all Doors revenue, but it was 1979 before all the loose ends were tied up and the parents started receiving any money.

Since then, Jim's share of the Doors' earnings have been worth several hundreds of thousands of dollars, at the peak more than a million dollars a year. Today, the Coursons have homes in Santa Barbara and Palm Springs and the Morrisons own substantial property in Orange and San Diego Counties. I think Jim would be amused that his posthumous fortune is being shared by a retired high school principal and a retired Navy admiral, authority figures for whom he had no time or respect when he was alive.

You can't get away with irony like that in fiction.

VII

WEIRD SCENES INSIDE THE GOLD MINE

BY 1973, there was someone in San Francisco who claimed to be (1) Jim Morrison, (2) Jim Morrison's reincarnation, or (3) someone who could put you in touch with Jim Morrison. The living room of his apartment had been turned into a shrine, with posters and fresh flowers brought in every day. Not long afterward, he was arrested for writing cheques in Jim's name.

In Los Angeles, one of the FM stations began playing a 'mystery tape' that sounded a near-perfect copy of Jim's voice and someone – it's not sure who – paid a visit to a journalist who had known Jim, so upsetting the journalist that he still won't say it was or wasn't the man he once interviewed.

Old girlfriends marched on New York publishers with poetry they claimed Jim had helped them write, as other publishers rejected memoirs and screenplays and novels by the score, all inspired by the Lizard King. And Elektra Records released another album, another repackaging of old hits, this one in quadrophonic sound.

In 1974, the mysterious, sound-alike tape was released by Capitol Records as a 45 rpm single by an artist identified only as 'Phantom'. An FBI voiceprint check in New York, requested by one of the radio stations, proved negative.

That's the way it's gone for 20 years. For a while, the grave was unmarked except by the fans, graffiti and trash, and when the Doors paid to have a marker made, it was promptly stolen.

On and on.

The *maitre d'* at the Ivy assured me that there was no reservation for anyone named Stone, and the impression I got was that the restaurant had more bookings per chair than a flight to Hawaii on United. I was early. I said I'd hang around for Oliver.

'Oliver?' the *maitre d'* asked. 'Oliver Stone, the director?' I nodded. 'Ah, well, then, of course, if Mr Stone comes, we can find a table, of course.'

Down the hall I saw Jim Morrison using the pay phone. I'd forgotten he was so tall. I laughed at myself. Morrison had been dead for nearly 20 years and this was Val Kilmer, the actor selected by Stone to play the sixties Lizard King. It was eerie. The start of principal photography was two months off, and Kilmer was already into the part: the leather wardrobe, the shaggy hair, the courtly manner, the boyish grin.

After Kilmer hung up the phone, I introduced myself and told him the *maitre d'* claimed there was no reservation. 'Not to worry,' said Kilmer, reaching for the phone again. He dialled Stone's office and said, 'Jerry and I are at the Ivy, and they say there's no reservation for Oliver. You better have somebody call down here and say Oliver Stone in a real loud voice right away.' No sooner had the phone been returned to the cradle than the *maitre d'* appeared and said, 'I can take you to your table now.'

At last. The Jim Morrison movie was really getting made. I had good reason to think it never would. I sold the movie rights to *No One Here Gets Out Alive* four times in seven years. That's probably no record, but in some circles in the 1980s, the Morrison story came to be regarded as one of those films that couldn't, or shouldn't, be made. Now that the project was finally under way – with Oliver Stone the writer-director – I looked back at the labyrinthine trail with some amazement. Over the years, dozens had been involved: Allan Carr, William Friedkin, Jerry Weintraub, Brian De Palma, Aaron Russo, Golan and Globus, Paul Schrader, Francis Coppola, Charlie Sheen, Irving Azoff, and Martin Scorsese among the directors and producers, and to play Morrison, John Travolta, Jason Patric, Keanu Reeves, Michael O'Keefe, Gregory Harrison, Michael Ontkean, Steven Bauer, Christopher Lambert, the lead singers from INXS (Michael Hutchence) and

U2 (Bono), Timothy Bottoms, Richard Gere, and Tom Cruise.

The story of the Doors movie is one of pissing contests and soaring egos, of complicated fuck-you option deals and people changing partners and sides, of Indians dancing on a Malibu beach and hundreds dancing on Morrison's grave. It is the story of parents and siblings, along with the surviving Doors and who knows how many agents and lawyers and other movie-biz types, all sides talking about karma and curses and the forces of evil and light, bickering over the Morrison myth and who has the right to do what with it.

Much of the early Morrison movie talk concerned making a documentary. In July 1981, on the tenth anniversary of Jim's death, a Boston film maker accompanied the surviving Doors to Paris, where they encountered a cluster of mournful fans gathered at Jim's grave. Witnesses say the band's keyboardist, Ray Manzarek, seized the moment as the cameras began to roll and climbed onto a nearby tombstone to make a fervent speech: 'Do you think Jim Morrison is here? I never saw the body! Jim's too big for this little grave, man! Do you really think he's dead?'

The Bostonian's documentary was not completed and a second try by a Hollywood film maker almost failed as well, until the Doors stepped in and assumed financial control. *A Tribute to Jim Morrison* runs an hour in length and blends new interviews with footage from concerts and the Doors' own early documentary, *Feast of Friends*.

Jim had been dead for nine years when my biography was published and when it topped *The New York Times* best-seller list and remained on that list for nine months, it was no surprise that Hollywood showed some interest. Rock and roll had been a key ingredient in several recent films, including *Saturday Night Fever* (1977), *Grease* and *The Buddy Holly Story* (both 1978), *The Rose* (1979) and the *Blues Brothers* (1980), all selling millions of albums as well as tickets.

In 1981, Sasha Harari, a recent immigrant from Israel, offered $50,000 for the film rights to my book. Harari then got *Grease* producer Allan Carr to write the cheque, with a second payment of $275,000 promised if the film went into production.

About the same time, the star of *Grease* and *Saturday Night Fever*, John Travolta, told Ray Manzarek that he wanted the film's lead role. Manzarek took Travolta on a crawl of Jim's favourite bars and actually talked about reuniting the Doors, with Travolta taking Morrison's place as vocalist. 'There was nothing around at the time that seemed as exciting to me,' Travolta said. 'The music was resurging, and I was really hot to do it.' The actor began rehearsing to Jim's videotapes, and he was good.

In 1981, with Allan Carr's $275,000 offer fresh in my fantasy, I was flown to California and put up in the choicest new hotel in Beverly Hills, L'Hermitage. A long, white limousine took me to Warner Bros., where the director of *The Exorcist* and *The French Connection*, William Friedkin, said he wanted me to write the script with Ray Manzarek. But the deal fell apart, and in Spring 1982, Allan Carr said I had dragged him into a fraudulent contract and demanded that I return the $50,000.

Three months later, *Rolling Stone* put Jim on the cover, the headline read, 'He's hot, he's sexy, and he's dead,' and the issue became one of the magazine's all-time best-sellers. Soon after that, Allan Carr offered a new contract and made another token payment, but it was a lost cause. The Doors had decided Carr didn't understand Jim, and as for Travolta, he was a nice guy, but Jim wasn't nice. Said drummer John Densmore, 'Jim was scary.'

Working with Travolta, director Brian De Palma began writing a script titled *Fire*, about a rock star who faked his death. Largely because *Eddie and the Cruisers*, a film that took a similar plot line, was in development, De Palma couldn't get a studio interested. Meanwhile, others approached Sasha Harari and the Doors, including Francis Coppola and Martin Scorsese, while Jim's sister Anne and her husband announced they were making a documentary *and* a feature film.

In 1985, Harari convinced the three Doors to renew their support, and the man who had promoted Doors concerts in San Francisco and New York in the 1960s, Bill Graham, was brought in to assist in negotiations with the Coursons and the Morrisons. By the time those talks were complete, the Coursons were promised that the movie would not be based on my book, which Mr Courson called a 'vile despicable rip-off', and that their daughter would not be shown having anything to do with the singer's death. In the agreement with the Morrisons, a clause specified that no mention of them would be made in the film; this was later altered to allow one, innocuous scene.

Harari called Oliver Stone's agent to ask if he'd be interested in directing the film. Harari was told he missed Stone by a day. Stone had just gone to the Philippines to make *Platoon*.

From 1985 to 1987, the project languished at Columbia Pictures, who subsequently dropped it when the studio got a new chairman. That was the year that *La Bamba* proved once again that a rock and roll story could work in film. More important, 1987 marked the twentieth anniversary of the 'Summer of Love', a media event that suggested a new psychedelic era might be standing in the wings – or, at the least, was worth a nostalgic look. United Artists and Warner Brothers showed interest in the Doors' story, but it went to Imagine Films, a company started by the actor Ron Howard following his success directing *Coccoon*. The efforts of the first screenwriter were rejected, however, and a second writer was given the assignment. That was when the Writers Guild went on strike in 1988.

In Hollywood there is something called *force majeure*, French for an 'Act of God'. As it is applied in Hollywood business practice, it can mean that if there is a writers' or directors' or actors' strike, all contracts in force at the time of the strike's beginning are extended for the length of the strike. When the writers' strike lasted six months, Imagine assumed its option on the Doors' life story and rights to the Doors' music were extended for a like period.

No way. It was a legally unsupportable tradition, said the Doors' legal representatives. It wasn't in writing and if Imagine didn't come up with $750,000 by 1 August 1988, when the option expired, all rights would revert to the Doors. Now, that may not seem a large figure by Hollywood standards, but Imagine had taken a terrible beating in the stock market crash the previous year and, according to some, the production company's cupboard was bare.

Producers and agents began circling. I started getting calls from Charlie Sheen, who said he wanted the movie rights and intended to produce the film and co-write a script on speculation with a friend, Scott Goldman. He said he had a production deal with Orion and U2's lead singer, Bono, was ready to play Morrison. At that time, Bono included a Doors medley in his band's performances.

'I've seen U2 in concert four times,' Sheen told me, 'and Bono does Morrison so fucking great, it's chilling. This is how it'll happen. We write the script in three weeks. Normally, I take ten days, but this is special. We send the script to you first, you tell me what you want. Sound good to you?' He told me to have my agent call his friend Goldman.

My agent did that and then called me and said, 'Goldman is 23, and everything I say, he says, "Oh, wow, that's really radical, what do we do now?"' I never heard from Sheen again.

The August deadline loomed and, at the final moment, who should come riding to Imagine's rescue but Carolco, the company that made its early fortune with the Rambo films. The Doors were paid $750,000, thus keeping the rights to the band's likenesses, story, and songs from reverting to the three surviving band members, the Coursons and the Morrisons. Once again, Jim belonged to Hollywood.

Still another screenwriter was hired, but his script was rejected, too. Oliver Stone claims he first became involved in discussions of a Doors movie as early as 1986 and now with his own two-picture deal in place at Carolco, Stone became firmly attached to the project. Stone devoured Jim's poetry and my book. He watched the Doors' video and film collection over and over again. He visited the scenes of the singer's life. He listened to the music constantly. Then he wrote a screenplay, in collaboration with J. Randal Johnson.

Soon after that, Oliver flew me to Los Angeles, where at the Ivy I met Val Kilmer. As we ordered the first glasses of wine, waiting for Stone to join us, I couldn't get over how much Kilmer looked like Morrison. From watching him as the renegade swordsman in *Willow*, I knew he had the right colouring, cheekbones, and muscled jaw. Now he was in character. Cowboy boots, hair the right length. He even blinked in precisely the same sleepy way that Morrison blinked and tilted his head shyly.

'I feel very lucky,' Kilmer said. 'Everybody wanted the part. Timothy Bottoms, Tom Cruise. Actors do the best they've ever done when they work with Oliver.'

We ordered more wine – of course we did, wasn't I drinking with Morrison again?—and I asked Kilmer how old he was. He told me he was 30. I said, 'You were just a kid in the sixties.'

He agreed, 'Yeah, I was, but I had an older brother who took me to a Jimi Hendrix concert and I've read a lot.' He asked if I had the original tapes of my interviews with Jim, because he wanted to copy Jim's voice.

If Kilmer bore surface similarities to Morrison, Stone's resemblance to the musician ran even deeper. They were only a couple of years apart in age, and they came from similar Establishment backgrounds. Stone's father was a Wall Street stockbroker, Morrison's a Navy officer. Both were college graduates. There was a common interest in writing and film; they experienced the world within verbal and visual contexts.

More important, I sensed a shared, anarchic intensity. There was a brash daring to experiment, coupled with a fierce determination to find emotional buttons and to push them hard. They liked to give people the finger, to test them. Getting a reaction was important.

Professionally, they looked for an audience's soft spots and attacked with guns and concepts blazing, or with such calculated control it was maddening. Oliver used great, looping, 360-degree pans that increased the pressure on the viewer in the same way that Jim inserted long silences into his songs. Oliver, as a writer, pulled a bloody head from a shoulder bag (*Year of the Dragon*), impaled a prison guard on a wall peg (*Midnight Express*), had the star throw his face into a heap of cocaine (*Scarface*), and, as the director of *Platoon*, had the good guy die with his arms out-thrust like the crucified Christ's. Jim posed for publicity pictures with an erection, frequently threw himself into the concert audience, vomited blood in one of rock's earliest videos, and in that notorious performance in Miami, dropped his pants at least part-way.

In Oliver, I sensed a volcano at rest. After he joined us at the table, I told him, 'When I first heard your name associated with the project, I thought: Stone's not particularly subtle, but neither was Jim. You're perfect for each other.' Stone showed his trademark gap-toothed grin.

Stone said he had a copy of a diary: a groupie's affair with the Shaman/Lizard King. He looked at Val and said, 'Everything is in there! This is a woman who was naked with Morrison many times! She talks about his cock! He's so gentle and loving. And then he turns into a complete shit. A complete Jekyll and Hyde.'

I returned to Los Angeles in May to watch a day's shooting as Stone's guest. The first thing I did was read the script, but Stone said I couldn't take it with me – I had to read it in an office at Carolco. I liked the script, as a script, but I was appalled by the liberties Stone had taken with both character and chronology. When Oliver's name was first attached to the Morrison film project, he was being criticized for the way he fictionalized Ron Kovic's life story in his film adaptation of Kovic's book, *Born on the Fourth of July*. Initially, Oliver denied the charges, but eventually he said he told 'small lies in order to reveal larger truths'. He went on to win the Oscar for Best Director for that film, but his reputation was sullied nonetheless, as he became cinema's answer to gonzo journalism, where you never let the facts get in the way of a good story. It appeared – at least in the script – that Stone was doing it again with what was then called 'The Doors Project'.

While it was true that Morrison was a sexual figure in practice as well as image – despite the impotence that plagued his last couple of years – the amount of sex in the script seemed disproportionate: more women dropped to their knees than you saw during an old-style Catholic Mass. Meg Ryan, who played Pam, absolutely refused to perform one of the scenes. (Even so, she showed her breasts and engaged in several vivid sexual performances.) When asked about Oliver's vision of Morrison, Val Kilmer said, 'It was tits and acid.'

Plus, Morrison's intelligence, gentlemanly manner, and

sense of humour were, to use a phrase Stone should recognize, missing in action.

I had a problem with the way Patricia Kennealy was portrayed. She was the magazine editor who had married Jim in a handfasting ceremony that was said to blend souls on a karmic and cosmic plane that has an effect on future incarnations of the two involved. Patricia happily agreed to play the part of the priestess who performed the handfasting. But when she arrived on the set to marry Val Kilmer to Kathleen Quinlan (who played the Kennealy part), she was given only the pages of her scene. When Stone warned her, 'I have you doing things in the script you didn't do,' she replied, 'That's okay, so long as they aren't things I wouldn't do.' She came to regret that.

After reading the script, I called her and told her that she had become three characters merged into one. For example, Oliver had her involved in a cocaine-induced blood orgy the first time that she and Jim met, when in reality they merely shook hands – while the orgy came late in Jim's life and involved a different woman [Magda].

In another scene, in a shower stall backstage at New Haven, Patricia asked Jim how much his father loved him. He held his fingers an inch apart. Patricia then asked how his mother felt. Jim held his fingers about an inch and a half apart. Patricia wasn't in New Haven, didn't meet Jim until much later, and told me that the entire scene was made up.

More important was Oliver's major theme: Morrison as shaman, the tribe's medicine man or priest. If Jim's tribe was the sixties generation, Oliver figured, surely Jim was the ecclesiastic. Didn't Jim himself say that the soul of a dying Indian leaped into his head at age five? As a college student, didn't he believe he could 'diagnose' an audience and devise a way to 'treat' it through manipulation? Didn't all those psychedelic drugs consumed during the sixties point in the same direction? Or was the shaman just another of Jim's images, like the Erotic Politician and the Lizard King?

When I saw Oliver the next day on the set, I asked him how it was going. He said it was hard. I looked puzzled, I guess, because he went on to explain that 'the shaman thing, it's going to be hard to get that across'.

I said, 'Yeah, you make a pretty big deal of it.'

He said, 'It's my hook. It's my hook.'

I asked Oliver, 'Was this always the way you felt about Jim?' He said yes, it was, even when he was in the jungle in Vietnam.

In the version of the film that reached the screen, the first scene shows the five-year-old Morrison encountering the dying Indian, and from that point forward there is a bald-headed Indian appearing in most of the important scenes, until in the final scene, just before Pam discovers Jim dead in the bathtub, the Indian is shown sneaking out of the bathroom and down the hall. There are flashbacks to the dying Indian, peyote rituals and hallucinations in the California desert, Indian drawings on the wall of a cave, ghost-like Indians dancing with Jim on the concert stage. Sorry, Oliver, but if that's your hook, I'm the fish that got away.

In another scene, Jim freaks out when he hears his band's biggest hit song, 'Light My Fire', used for a car commercial, when in reality, Jim stopped Chrysler or Buick or whoever it was from using the song (after the other Doors signed over the rights without him) and the commercial never happened. I could go on.

And yet, all of these changes were made while painstaking attention was being paid to re-creating the smallest environmental detail. When I told Robby Krieger that Oliver's office had called me repeatedly to determine precisely when certain pictures in my book were taken, to establish accurate wardrobe chronology, he admitted that the wardrobe was flawless. When Patricia Kennealy was flown to Hollywood to perform the handfasting, she found that her New York apartment had been duplicated so perfectly that she saw bills bearing her Lower East Side address on the desk.

And the truth is, most of the film is accurate, most of the events depicted did occur more or less as written and filmed. And it appears that millions of dollars were spent replicating not only the Whisky a Go-Go and the sixties concert halls (with up to 3,000 extras in attendance), but also the Sunset Strip and the Haight-Ashbury section of San Francisco. As someone who was there, let me say that Oliver really took me back, whip-lashing me through my past with stunning accuracy. And if the Ed Sullivan, Andy Warhol, and Truman Capote characters in the film appeared to be made of *papier maché*, Val Kilmer as Jim was bang-on. He looked like Jim, he talked and sang like Jim, and he moved like Jim. The film was, in fact, a one-man tour de force.

Unfortunately, the script did not give Val Kilmer the dimension that Jim deserved, and that history demanded. Oh, Jim was portrayed accurately enough, but only up to a point. Oliver's 'take' on Jim showed him to be a mean, self-indulgent, self-destructive drunk. All true, of course. But he also was charming, witty, intelligent, articulate, and he had a sense of humour about himself. I believe the interviews in this book and, I hope, in a few of the stories I've told, a fuller, more accurate portrait emerges. Oliver's movie gives a narrow, ugly picture. When Jim finally lifted the last bottle to his lips, and drained it, many in the film's audience were quite content to see him go take a bath. As I left the theatre after one viewing, I heard someone say, 'I couldn't wait for that sonofabitch to die.' I went home feeling as if Oliver had betrayed Jim. I don't think Jim should be held up as a role model for younger generations. But when you trash a man as thoroughly as Oliver Stone trashed Jim Morrison in *The Doors*, the good stuff that Jim had to say gets trashed as well.

I remember the sixties – and Jim – as being more fun. I remember that there was more hope. Looking back now, we may seem to have been naive, but there was an innocence and optimism that Oliver missed. Maybe it's because he was in Vietnam at the time, losing his.

Maybe so and maybe not. Sure enough, the Doors had a dark side. And everyone is entitled to his or her 'take' on Jim's life. More than anyone else I've known or met, Jim was like the elephant described by a group of blind men; each blind man, grabbing a different piece of the elephant's anatomy, inevitably described it differently. So if this is what Oliver Stone saw in his mind's eye, if Oliver wants to fictionalize Jim's life, and turn him into an Indian shaman, why not? Because Jim did the same thing. I just think that Oliver made a bigger deal of it than Jim ever did.

I believe that from an early age, at least from adolescence, Jim thought of himself in larger-than-life proportions. Most people in high school struggle to find their identity. Jim wanted something more; he wanted to create it. As a student at Clearwater Junior College, at Florida State University, and at UCLA, he continued his self-creation. As a rock star in the sixties, his fantasies were introduced to an audience that wanted to believe anything and everything. Revolt and getting back at your parents. Death. Sex. Drugs. Rock and roll. Themes for an eternity.

Following one of the entertainment business's Golden Rules, Jim gave them what they wanted.

And what of his enduring popularity?

Jim followed another Golden Rule: he left his audience wanting more.

THE
INTERVIEWS

LOS ANGELES
FREE PRESS
John Carpenter
Summer 1968

John Carpenter was the music editor of the *Los Angeles Free Press*, a weekly 'underground' newspaper distributed throughout Southern California. Like Jim, he was a big drinker, and the interview stretched over all of one day, starting with a breakfast laced with Bloody Marys and ending in the Phone Booth, Jim's favourite topless bar.

As detailed earlier, in the biographical section of this book, John took the transcript of the tape to Jim for approval. Jim added some clarification and Pamela took a blue pencil to the interview, slashing uncounted hundreds of paragraphs where she felt Jim was making an ass of himself. The interview survived her editing, revealing Jim's robust delight in life.

JOHN CARPENTER: *How did the cover on* Strange Days *come about?*
JIM MORRISON: I hated that cover on the first album. So I said, 'I don't want to be on this cover. Where is that? Put a chick on it or something. Let's have a dandelion or a design.' The title, *Strange Days* came and everybody said yeah, 'cause that was where we were, what was happening. It was so right.

Originally I wanted us in a room surrounded by about 30 dogs, but that was impossible 'cause we couldn't get the dogs and everybody was saying, 'What do you want dogs for?' And I said that it was symbolic that it spelled God backwards. *[Laughs]* Finally we ended up leaving it up to the art director and the photographer. We wanted some real freaks though, and he came out with a typical side show thing. It looked European. It was better than having our fucking faces on it though.

What place do albums have as art forms to you?
I believe they've replaced books. Really. Books and movies. They're better than movies 'cause a movie you see maybe once or twice, then later on television maybe. But a fucking album man, it's more influential than any art form going. Everybody digs them. They've got about 40 of them in their houses and some of them you listen to 50 times, like the Stones' albums or Dylan's.

You don't listen to the Beatles much anymore, but there are certain albums that just go on and on. You measure your progress mentally by your records, like when you were really young what you had then, Harry Belafonte, you know, Calypso, Fats Domino, Elvis Presley.

You guys are only working weekends now, aren't you?
No, not really. I think we work a lot. More than most people think. Like after the [Hollywood] Bowl we go to Texas, then to Vancouver, Seattle, then jump to the East Coast, Montreal and blah, blah, blah. Take three weeks off in August for the film, then we go to Europe. Man, we work an awful lot!

Do you still read a lot?
No, not as much as I used to. I'm not as prolific a writer either. Like when, a while ago, I was living in this abandoned office building, sleeping on the roof, you know the tale. *[Laughs]* And all of a sudden, I threw away all my notebooks that I'd been keeping since high school and these songs just kept coming

to me. Something about the moon, I don't remember.

Well, I'd have to make up words as fast as I could in order to hold onto the melody – you know a lot of people don't know it, but I write a lot of the melodies too – later, all that would be left would be the words 'cause I couldn't hold on to them. The words were left in a sort of vague idea. In those days when I heard a song, I heard it as an entire performance. Taking place, you know, with the audience, the band and the singer. Everything. It was kind of like a prediction of the future. It was all there.

How did the ending to 'The End' come about? Is the Whisky a Go-Go story true?

I used to have this magic formula, like, to break into the subconscious. I would lay there and say over and over 'Fuck the mother, kill the father. Fuck the mother, kill the father.' You can really get into your head just repeating that slogan over and over. Just saying it can be the thing . . .

That mantra can never become meaningless. It's too basic and can never become just words 'cause as long as you're saying it, you can never be unconscious. That all came from up here.

That really shook the Whisky audience up when you did it. Have you ever really gotten through to an audience like the first time you went over and got mobbed and all?

Not like the thing that's in my mind. I think the day that thing happens it will be all over. The End. Where would you go from there? If everyone, even for a split second, became one. They could never come back. No, I don't think it can ever happen, not like it is in my head.

My audiences . . .they usually get pretty turned on. It's like saying at first you're the audience and we're up here, you're down there. Then all of a sudden there you are and you're right there just like us . . . it's out of sight. When they know 'You're just like us,' it breaks down all the barriers and I like that a lot.

I've heard a lot of talk from friends in England, and some of the groups from there, that a lot of hostility will be aimed your way when you go over there. You know, as America's super-sex group and all.

Yeah? . . . hmmm, there's gonna be a bit of hostility, huh? That's a good prediction, yeah, a prediction of the future. There is going to be a little bit of hostility and if there isn't, I'm going to be a little bit disappointed. The more hostility, the better. *[Laughs]* Opposition is true friendship, ha!

[Knock on the door. It's the maid.]

Come on in, we're splitting anyway.

The Lizard King

MAID: *I'm ready if you are, [Waits] I'm ready if you are . . . I know you like a clean bed. [Leaves room to get cleaning materials.]*

I knew this was going to be good, but not that good. Let's split right after we hear what else she has to say. *[Laughs]*

MAID: *I'm ready for you if you're ready for me.*

Come here for a little peace and quiet and everyone keeps pushing me.

MAID: *Is that right? [Laughs] Yeah, just keeps on doin' it. Well, I'm ready for you if you're ready for me. [Hums]*

Please, no singing, this is a holiday. I'm on holiday.

[In the elevator.]

Where were you living a year ago?

A year ago? At the Tropicana. Yeah, I started that whole scene. Put it on the map. We used to have lots of fun there. Yeah, it's boisterous. Them [the band] was there, nice guys.

[In the street on the way to the Doors' office. Sunset to Santa Monica on foot.]

Man, I really feel good.

You had your album all ready to go and you went back into the studio to add some things, then I hear you left if alone.

Yeah, we didn't do it. I was going to add some poetry where the little space is between the cuts. But who wants to listen to some cat talking. The music is what's happening. That's what they want to hear. Anybody can talk, but how many cats can play music and sing?

It seems strange to walk in L.A.

Yeah, doesn't it man! *[Bike rider yells, honks, U-turns]* Who was that? It's Babe *[the Doors' road manager].*

BABE: *Where you headed, the office? [Babe goes on ahead on his bike.]*

He's a happy cat, you know? He's either a genius or really dumb, I haven't found out which. He sure knows how to have a good time. A happy cat.

Oh, there was this chick once, you know, at a concert. She came back stage and said that there was this person that wanted to meet me. She said it was her friend and she was deaf and dumb so I went through this number, you know, drawing pictures, sign language, and it turns out she was putting me on. *[Laughs]*

I really dig L.A. IN THE SUMMER. Winters are a drag, but Summer's pretty nice.

I really dig L.A. Really a lot.

[Topless bar. Babe joins us, drinks are there.]

[To Babe] Dig you, big drinker.

BABE: *[Indicating a dancer.] Can you imagine the babies that chick could have?*

That's bad for their tits when they dance topless. Ask any topless dancer. If they lose them it would be like losing your head . . . She doesn't work too hard. Just sort of stands there . . . Bless this house and all that are in it.

[Later]

[Pointing to new dancer] She's too satirical. She doesn't take anything seriously. I get the feeling that if you spent a lot of time in a place like this you'd corrupt your soul. Corrode it completely. But let's hold off that. Can you imagine bringing your secretary in here? Ha!

['If I Were a Carpenter' by the Four Tops on juke]

If I were a carpenter and you were a lady, would you marry me anyway?

BABE: *No. No. If you were a good natured prostitute I might, maybe. Everybody knows that prostitutes make the best wives, Henry Miller taught us that, right, John?*

Henry who? [To Morrison] What do you think about what's been print-ed about you and the stuff you hear back all the time? Did you read the Post *magazine thing?*

Yeah, I read it. You know, I knew she was going to do it that way. Journalists are people, you know, and the chicks . . . she did a number, man. Yeah, if you don't really come on to them, they feel neglected, you know? She ended up doing a number. It was written good though. You really felt like you were there. It lies a lot of times. I hear things back all the time that I'm supposed to have done.

Hey, Babe, you're gonna be a famous person one of these days and you should learn to hold your tongue. Especially in front of the press. How'd you like to wake up one day and you've said something off the top of your head and have to read about it the next day, like that is supposed to be where you're at.

The mentality of the writer is like the 'psychology' of the voyeur. Journalists never seem to speak about themselves like other people do. They absorb like a sponge and never really discuss their own psyche. I think that . . . like . . . I think art, which is like beauty, is the revelation of beauty, beauty is an absolute, you dig? And I think it's rooted in a disinterested perception of the real world. Striking an evenness, a balance between object and receiver, like revealing the world with no connotation at all. None, no bullshit.

You know when you've done it, and if you haven't, you are still on the way. But me, if I get something really good, I'm gonna lay it out, do you dig? But a lot of it gets into that 'He was standing there on the street step with his eyeball exposed.' My perspective when people ask me questions is like I tell them where it's at over and over and over again. Me, me, me . . . But then that's only part of it, part of the thing; not the whole answer.

There's a little more to it than that. Yeah, like I think that there is a sub-world in which everybody is sleeping. This whole other world that everybody's trying to forget, but which we remember, immediately everybody knows it. But people love the game. The Game. They really dig it and nobody is supposed to admit that it's a game. They won't. If they did, then they would ruin the game.

In the middle of the baseball game, like if someone ran out and said, 'It's a game, man, just a fucking game, this is fucked. Are you kidding me? It's just a fucking game.' Well, everybody would say, 'Wow, man, get that fucking clown out of here.' They'd go home, eat a big meal, ball their old lady, and then be right there. He who laughs last, laughs his ass off.

BABE: *Can you dig that? Do you know what he's saying? I think you're serious. I haven't been able to dig it completely yet, but it's there. I know it's there.*

[Later]

It's weird. People in here, after the initial glimpse, just start going on their own trips, talking, eating, drinking. Do you know what it is? I bet that was the appeal of the brothel. Like the atmosphere, a place for conversation.

Man, this is the place I'd really like to work, only instead of business men, it would be business women, you know, just stopping by for a little drink before . . . I must say, she is my favourite. She's out of sight . . . I think it's a mistake to have their breasts exposed. An error in theatrics. They should be wearing some thin negligee. Mystery . . .

BABE: *That's what turns me off to some of the hippie chicks. I guess I'm old fashioned enough to still want some femininity and expect a little mystery. But those chicks in Levis and scraggly hair really turn me off.*

I like chicks in Levis. My taste is like whoever approaches me, I think it's groovy.

Sounds pretty exhausting.

BABE: *You know what's a groovy word? Bell-wether: leader of a mind-less crowd. That's what you are, Jim. The leader of a mindless crowd.*

Babe, that's what I mean. You got to learn to curb your tongue. I can see what it will be like. John would say, 'and then Babe said you know what you are Jim? The leader of a mindless crowd.' If you print that, John, I won't kill you, I'll haunt you. They all have minds.

Maybe collectively . . . a crowd together really has no mind. Individually everybody does. They all have bitchin' minds. Like, I bet there's more philosophy in some sixteen-year-old chick's mind than you ever dreamed of in your whole cigarette. Some of those letters to those fan magazines are really lonely and deep and open. Some of them are bullshit. I don't read many, but some that I've read really knocked me out. Really open, sincere. Anyway, you got to learn to hold your tongue. Can you remember that?

BABE: *I'll remember that. I'll keep silent like deep water. Whenever I say anything from now on, it will be such a profundity that you guys will just fall out of your chairs.*

WAITRESS: *That will be $39.75.*

W N E T - T V
C R I T I Q U E
Richard Goldstein
Spring 1969

This was the first interview after the Miami concert,
conducted in a television studio in New York.
The interviewer was Richard Goldstein, a writer for the
Village Voice who previously interviewed Jim
in 1968 for *New York* magazine. The interview
was a brief one, coupled with a live
performance by the Doors.

The Lizard King

OK, let's talk about the Doors. They begin at U.C.L.A. where Morrison and Manzarek are enrolled in a Master's programme in film-making; they share a house in Venice, California, near the beach. Ray introduces his friends Krieger and Densmore to Jim's poetry; they begin to jam together at small clubs on the Sunset Strip and even in their early tapes there's a distinct bluesy feeling, which sometimes gets lost in the poetics but usually comes out in the rhythm, where it counts. Anyway, a huge record company signs them, then changes its mind, another company grabs them up and this time they record. Their first album sells more copies than My Weekly Reader; *they become superstars, able to leap tall groupies in a single bound, able to fill any hall in the western world. They garner as much publicity from their presence as they do from their music. This seems to put the authorities uptight but it delights the kids. It's like Jim Morrison once said: 'When you make your peace with authority you become an authority'. I interviewed the Doors when they were in town a few weeks ago and I'd like to run some of that tape for you now.*

JIM MORRISON: I think in a way rock concerts have always served a function. It gives a lot of people, with the same station in life, a chance to gather together and kind of assemble and just feel the sheer mass of them that exists, that the numbers . . .

RICHARD GOLDSTEIN: *I think that's a good point*

RAY MANZAREK: On the other hand you can take 10,000 people coming together and there's a sense of communion, a communal thing; we're all here together and there's no reason. A lot of energy is dissipated in the concert, but there's no reason that that same communal thing can't be taken out into the outside world and ideally, hopefully, that's what a rock, a good rock concert can do. People are together inside and they get outside into the parking lot and start driving home, and get into their homes. I hope they still realise that they're together – you know, they were together in the concert, and they're together in their homes, they're together in their schools, they're together on the street. And if the people can work that togetherness and keep that thing going, working it, and working it, eventually, everything's going to turn out alright.

You get a community feeling.

[Yeah]

A contact high, so to speak . . . I once wrote a piece on you called The Shaman as Superstar *in which I suggested that rock musicians, rock heroes, perform a religious function for young people. Do you sometimes see your concerts as a sort of ritual?*

JIM MORRISON: It's a funny thing . . . I've read a little bit about shamanism. I haven't seen too much of it first hand, except you know, what we see with the music and that kind of thing, but in, er, tribes the shaman can be any age, can be an old man, or a young man, but the whole tribe, all ages, kind of try to push him into his trip and listen to him, irregardless [*sic*]. It was just a question of a certain psychological tendency in the individual.

What do you think the role is of say, a rock shaman in a time of social turmoil, with kids taking things into their own hands more or less.

JIM MORRISON: I don't think the shaman from what I've read, is really too interested in defining his role in society. He's just more interested in pursuing his own fantasies. If he became too self-conscious of a function, you know, I think it might tend to ruin his own inner trip.

Do you think that's why a lot of rock people have been reluctant to get involved in issue-oriented politics, you know, make statements on the school crisis and what have you?

JIM MORRISON: A lot of people just aren't interested in politics at all.

Well, as you go round the world, as you travel, through Europe and America, what do kids look for as far as projecting through you?

JOHN DENSMORE: Its funny – in Europe the kids were much more politically-oriented, you know. If we said anything politically they'd go into a furore. I mean they love it, especially anything against America, you know. If we just played they dug that too, but they really dug the political side of it, but in America it's just the opposite really. A lot of people at our concerts at least, they're sort of, it seems like they don't really come to hear us speak politics.

What do they come to hear?

JOHN DENSMORE: I think they come more for the religious experience.

How does that translate in terms of rhythm, riffs and things like that?

RAY MANZAREK: You really can't, because any rhythm, any riff, any sort of lyric is a release, you know, you're releasing yourself totally into whatever you happen to be playing at the moment.

How about in lyrics? What's the difference between a rock lyric and a poem?

RAY MANZAREK: Well, there's really no difference, you know.

213

Jim's book is the same as Jim's lyrics. I can read a page and I've heard him sing pretty much the same things. You know for him I don't think it's any difference at all – this is written poetry and what he does on stage is spoken poetry. His spoken poetry is very effective, although some poems read better than they speak, but for the most part, spoken poetry is much more effective.

JOHN DENSMORE: What we do sometimes is like we'll play a song and we'll play the structure of the song and then we'll get into a free part and we'll improvise musically and he'll improvise lyrically and that will probably be just straight poetry, you know, and then we'll get back into the form later.

It would naturally seem much more fluid than what you've got in the book then.

JIM MORRISON: A lot of our most interesting songs develop over a period of time playing night after night in clubs. We'd start out into a fairly basic song and then the music would settle into a kind of hypnotic river of sound which would leave me free to kind of make up anything that came into my head at the time. I like songs but that's the part of the performance that I enjoy the most, to pick up vibrations from the music and what's coming from the audience and, er, just kind of follow it wherever it goes.

How does that differ from when you write a poem?

JIM MORRISON: It's very similar. I think a lot of poetry is very close to music except when you write a poem often you just, you have to be in a state of mind that music can put you in, with its hypnotic quality that leaves you free, you know just to let the subconscious play itself out wherever it goes. I really admire poets who can get up with or without a microphone just in front of a group of people and start reciting their poetry. I really admire that. But I find the music gives me a kind of security and it makes it a lot easier to express myself or else, it's kind of hard just to read it dry. I wish I could, I'd like to work on that a little bit more.

I think that one of the trends which are pretty evident in rock now is that it's becoming demystified. The mystery is being extracted and we're getting very concerned with words like honest music, down-home music, and things like that, you know. How does this affect your stuff?

JIM MORRISON: I was talking about that this weekend, thinking a lot about it. I think the two basic types of music indigenous to this country are the black music, blues, and the kind of folk music that was brought over from Europe, I guess they call it country music or the kind of West Virginia High and Lonesome sound. Those are the two mainstreams of root American music, and there might be others around, but it looks like ten years ago what they called rock'n'roll was kind of a blending of those two forms. I guess what's happening now is that rock is kinda dying out and everyone's going back to their roots again. Some are going back into country and some are going back into basic blues. I guess in four or five years, the new generation's music will have a synthesis of those two elements and some third thing that will entire . . . maybe it'll be, it might rely heavily on electronics, er, tapes . . . I can kind of envision maybe one person with a lot of machines, tapes and electronic set-ups, singing or speaking and using machines.

I used to think that rock was progressing, you know, that there's a line from some point to another. But instead it's a wave, really, and there's a return to . . .

JIM MORRISON: That's why I like blues and jazz musicians, country musicians, they just keep on exploring their own music. Sometimes they're right on time and the public finds something in it that expresses the time, and sometimes they're out of favour, but I think for musicians and poets, artists in general, just to keep exploring their own field and if you're popular go with it, and if you go out of favour just keep doing it, you know.

ROLLING STONE
Jerry Hopkins
Spring 1969

After the disastrous Miami concert, *Rolling Stone*
magazine put Jim's face on its cover as part of a wanted
poster, while the stories more or less portrayed him as a
drunken fool. I believed that while he may have been
that, he also possessed an intelligence that had been
overlooked. I suggested to Jann Wenner that we
interview Jim in depth.

Initially, Jim was somewhat reluctant to be interviewed,
but he changed his mind and we met off and on over a
period of two weeks, over lunch, over drinks, and
between visits to his favourite topless bars. At all times,
he was well-behaved, thoughtful, articulate. It appeared
to me that he was trying to balance the earlier coverage.

The interview was published in *Rolling Stone*
and later was collected in a volume of *Rolling Stone*
interviews, which is now out of print.

The Lizard King

The week I interviewed Jim Morrison, the Doors were being banned from performing in St. Louis and Honolulu because of exhibitionism and drunkenness charges filed against Morrison following a concert in Miami – yet, it was the same week that Morrison finished writing a screenplay with poet Michael McClure and signed a contract with Simon and Schuster for his own first book of poetry.

Unlike the mythology, the music of the Doors remains a constant – a force which has not been so much an 'influence' in rock, but a monument. 'The music is your special friend.' Morrison sang in 'The Music's Over' and for millions, the music of the Doors is just that; just as the Beatles' 'Sgt. Pepper' renders a generation weak with nostalgia, so does the Doors' 'Light My Fire.' At the group's peak, in 1967–68, there was also a strident urgency about Morrison's music. 'We want the world and we want it now.'

Morrison was somewhat reluctant to be interviewed by Rolling Stone *at first, believing the publication's coverage of the Miami concert and aftermath had made him seem a clown. Finally he changed his mind and in sessions that rambled over more than a week and several neighbourhood drinking spots, he proved his manager Bill Siddons correct when Siddons said, 'Jim used to have a lot of little demons inside him . . . but I don't think he has so many anymore.' In other words, Morrison had mellowed, matured. Still he was playful – 'This is really a strange way to make a living, isn't it?' he said one day – but he was also trying to get people to take him seriously. All poets wish to be taken seriously, but many also have acted in a style that would seem to contradict or destroy this wish.*

The first session we met at the Doors' office (which is convenient to both the Elektra office and several topless clubs) and talked in a neighbourhood bar called the Palms. The idea was to get some lunch with the beer, but the cook was out for the day so it was just beer – with a small group of regulars scattered along the bar buying each other rounds and telling noisy stories in the background, while we sat at a small table nearby. There was no perceptible notice paid Morrison when he entered, and the full beard he had grown since Miami had little to do with it; he was a regular here, too.

JERRY HOPKINS: *How did you decide you were going to be a performer?*

JIM MORRISON: I think I had a suppressed desire to do something like this ever since I heard . . . y'see, the birth of rock'n'roll coincided with my adolescence, my coming into awareness. It was a real turn-on, although at the time I could never allow myself to rationally fantasise about doing it myself. I guess all that time I was unconsciously accumulating inclination and listening. So when it finally happened, my subconscious had prepared the whole thing.

I didn't think about it. It was just there. I never did any singing. I never even conceived it. I thought I was going to be a writer or a sociologist, maybe write plays. I never went to concerts – one or two at most. I saw a few things on TV, but I'd never been part of it all. But I heard in my head a whole concert situation, with a band singing and an audience – a large audience. Those first five or six songs I wrote, I was just taking notes at a fantastic rock concert that was going on inside my head. And once I had written the songs, I had to sing them.

When was this?

About three years ago. I wasn't in a group or anything. I just got out of college and I went down to the beach. I wasn't doing much of anything. I was free for the first time. I had been going to school, constantly, for fifteen years. It was a beautiful hot summer, and I just started hearing songs. I think I still have the notebook with those songs written in it. This kind of mythic concert that I heard . . . I'd like to try and reproduce it sometime, either in actuality or on record. I'd like to reproduce what I heard on the beach that day.

Had you ever played any musical instrument?

When I was a kid I tried piano for a while, but I didn't have the discipline to keep up with it.

How long did you take piano?

Only a few months. I think I got to about the third-grade book.

Any desire now to play an instrument?

Not really. I play maracas. I can play a few songs on the piano. Just my own inventions, so it's not really music; it's noise. I can play one song. But it's got only two changes in it, two chords, so it's pretty basic stuff. I would really like to be able to play guitar, but I don't have the feeling for it. [*Pause*] You play any?

No . . .

I read a book you did – *The Hippie Papers*. It had some nice articles in it. I've thought of writing for the underground press, because I don't know anywhere else you can have an idea one day and see it in print almost immediately. I'd like to write a column for under-ground newspapers. Just reporting things I see. Not fiction, but reporting. Just trying to get accurate reports on things I witness – around L.A. especially. I guess I'm afraid of wasting a lot of good ideas on journalism. If I kept them in my head long enough they might really turn into something. Although there've been some good people writing as journalists – Dickens, Dostoevski . . . and of course Mailer is a contemporary journalist.

Mailer even turned out a novel, a chapter a month under deadline for Esquire . . .

And it's brilliant. *The American Dream*. Probably one of the best novels in the last decade.

It's interesting . . . a lot of good stuff is conceived specifically for news-papers and magazines, just as a lot of good music is conceived for records – all of which are disposable items, things which are available to just about anyone for very little money and later thrown away or traded in or gotten rid of pretty quickly. It's making several art forms very temporary . . .

That's why poetry appeals to me so much – because it's so eternal. As long as there are people, they can remember words and combinations of words. Nothing else can survive a holocaust, but poetry and songs. No one can remember an entire novel. No one can describe a film, a piece of sculpture, a painting. But so long as there are human beings, songs and poetry can continue.

When did you start writing poetry?

Oh, I think around the fifth or sixth grade I wrote a poem called 'The Pony Express'. That was the first I can remember. It was one of those ballad-type poems. I never could get it together, though. I always wanted to write, but I figured it'd be no good unless somehow the hand just took the pen and started moving without me really having anything to do with it. Like, automatic writing. But it just never happened. I wrote a few poems, of course.

Like 'Horse Latitudes' I wrote when I was in high school. I kept a lot of notebooks through high school and college, and then when I left school for some dumb reason – maybe it was wise – I threw them all away. There's nothing I can think of I'd rather have in my possession right now than those two or three lost notebooks. I was thinking of being hypnotised or taking sodium pentathol to try to remember, because I wrote in those books night after night. But maybe if I'd never thrown them away, I'd never have written anything original – because they were mainly accumulations of things that I'd read or heard, like quotes from books. I think if I'd never gotten rid of them I'd never have been free.

Do you have songs you like better than others?

I tell you the truth, I don't listen to the stuff much. There are songs I enjoy doing more in person than others. I like singing the blues – these free, long blues trips where there's no specific beginning or end. It just gets into a groove, and I can just keep making up things. And everybody's soloing. I like that kind of song rather than just a *song*. You know, just starting on a blues and just seeing where it takes us.

Improvisational trips . . .

Yeah. We needed another song for this album. We were racking our brains trying to think what song. We were in the studio, and so we started throwing out all these old songs. Blues trips. Rock classics. Finally we just started playing and we played for about an hour, and we went through the whole history of rock music – starting with blues, going through rock'n'roll, surf music, Latin, the whole thing. I call it 'Rock Is Dead.' I doubt if anybody'll ever hear it.

You were quoted recently as saying you thought rock was dead. Is this something you really believe?

It's like what we were talking about earlier in the movement back to the roots. The initial flash is over. The thing they call rock, what used to be called rock'n'roll – it got decadent. And then there was a rock revival sparked by the English. That went very far. It was articulate. Then it became self-conscious, which I think is the death of any movement. It became self-conscious, involuted and kind of incestuous. The energy is gone. There is no longer a belief.

I think that for any generation to assert itself as an aware human entity, it has to break with the past, so obviously the kids that are coming along next are not going to have much in common with what we feel. They're going to create their own unique sound. Things like wars and monetary cycles get involved too. Rock'n'roll probably could be explained by . . . it was after the Korean War was ended . . . and there was a psychic purge. There seemed to be a need for an underground explosion, like an eruption. So maybe after the Vietnam War is over – it'll probably take a couple of years maybe; it's hard to say – but it's possible that the deaths will end in a couple of years, and there will again be a need for a life force to express itself, to assert itself.

Do you feel you'll be part of it?

Yeah, but I'll probably be doing something else by then. It's hard to say. Maybe I'll be a corporation executive . . .

Have you ever thought of yourself in that role – seriously?

I kinda like the image. Big office. Secretary . . .

How do you see yourself? Poet? Rock Star? What?

I don't get too much feedback except what I read. I like to read things that are written about it. That's the only time I get any kind of feedback on the whole thing. Living in L.A., it's no big deal. It's an anonymous city, and I live an anonymous life. Our group never reached the mass phenomenon stage that some did, either; there never was the mass adulation. So it never really got to me much. I guess I see myself as a conscious artist plugging away from day to day, assimilating information. I'd like to get a theatre going of my own. I'm very interested in that now. Although I still enjoy singing.

A question you've been asked before, countless times: do you see yourself in a political role? I'm throwing a quote of yours back at you, in which you described the Doors as 'erotic politicians'.

It was just that I've been aware of the national media while growing up. They were always around the house, and so I started reading them. And so I became aware gradually, just by osmosis, of their style, their approach to reality. When I got into the music field, I was interested in securing kind of a place in that world, and so I was turning keys, and I just knew instinctively how to do it. They look for catchy phrases and quotes they can use for captions, something to base an article on to give it an immediate response. It's the kind of term that does mean something, but it's impossible to explain. If I tried to explain what it means to me, it would lose all its force as a catchword.

Deliberate media manipulation, right? Two questions come to me. Why did you pick that phrase over others? And do you think it's pretty easy to manipulate the media?

I don't know if it's easy, because it can turn on you. But, well, that was just one reporter, y'see. I was just answering his question. Since then a lot of people have picked up on it – that phrase – and have made it pretty heavy, but actually I was just . . . I knew the guy would use it, and I knew what the picture painted would be. I knew that a few key phrases is all anyone ever retains from an article. So I wanted a phrase that would stick in the mind.

I do think it's more difficult to manipulate TV and film than it is the press. The press has been easy for me in a way, because I am biased toward writing, and I understand writing and the mind of writers; we are dealing with the same medium, the printed word. So that's been fairly easy. But television and films are much more difficult, and I'm still learning. Each time I go on TV I get a little more relaxed and a little more able to communicate openly, and control it. It's an interesting process.

Does this explain your fascination with film?

I'm interested in film because to me it's the closest approximation in art that we have to the actual flow of consciousness, in both dream life and in the everyday perception of the world.

You're getting more involved in film all the time . . .

Yeah, but there's only one we've completed – *Feast of Friends*, which was made at the end of a spiritual, cultural renaissance that's just about over now. It was like what happened at the end of the plague in Europe that decimated half the population. People danced, they wore colourful clothing. It was a kind of incredible springtime. It'll happen again, but it's over, and the film was made at the end of it.

I think of one part of the film, a performance sequence, in which you're flat on your back, still singing . . . which represents how theatrical you've gotten in your performance. How did this theatricality develop? Was it a conscious thing?

I think in a club, histrionics would be a little out of place, because the room is too small and it would be a little grotesque. In a large concert situation, I think it's just . . . necessary, because it gets to be more than just a musical event. It turns into a little bit of a spectacle. And it's different every time. I don't think any one performance is like any other. I can't answer that very well. I'm not too conscious of what's happening. I don't like to be too objective about it. I like to let each thing happen – direct it a little consciously, maybe, but just kind of follow the vibrations I get in each particular circumstance. We don't plan theatrics. We hardly ever know which set we'll play.

You mentioned that there were certain songs you liked performing over others, those which allow you some room for improvisation. I assume you mean pieces like 'The End' and 'The Music's Over' . . .

Once they got on record, they became very ritualised and static. Those were kind of constantly changing free-form pieces but once we put them on record, they just kind of stopped. They were kind of at the height of their effect anyway, so it didn't really matter. No . . . I mean the kind of songs where the musicians just start jamming. It starts off with a rhythm, and you don't know how it's going to be or really what it's about, until it's over. That sort I enjoy best.

When you're writing material, do you consciously differentiate between a poem, something for print . . . and a song lyric, something to be sung?

To me a song comes with the music, a sound or rhythm first, then I make up words as fast as I can just to hold onto the feel – until actually the music and the lyric come almost simultaneously. With a poem, there's not necessarily any music . . .

But usually a sense of rhythm, though . . .

Right. Right. A sense of rhythm and, in that sense, a kind of music. But a song is more primitive. Usually has a rhyme and a basic meter, whereas a poem can go anywhere.

Well, who provides this musical line that you hear when you're writing? The band? Or is this something you hear inside your head?

Well, most songs I've written just came. I'm not a very prolific songwriter. Most of the songs I've written I wrote in the very beginning, about three years ago. I just had a period when I wrote a lot of songs.

In the first three albums, writer credit in every song goes to the Doors, as opposed to individuals. But I understand that in the next album individual writers will be listed. Why?

In the beginning, I wrote most of the songs, the words and music. On each successive album, Robby [Krieger] contributed more songs. Until finally on this album it's almost split between us.

A lot of the songs in the beginning, me or Robby would come in with a basic idea, words and melody. But then the whole arrangement and actual generation of the piece would happen night after night, day after day, either in rehearsals or in clubs. When we became a concert group, a record group, and when we were contracted to provide so many albums a year, so many singles every six months, that natural, spontaneous, generative process wasn't given a chance to happen as it had in the beginning. We actually had to create songs in the studio. What started to happen was Robby or I would just come in with a song and the arrangement already completed in our minds, instead of working it out slowly.

Do you think your work has suffered because of this?

Yeah. If we did nothing but record, it probably would be all right. But we do other things, too, so there's not the time to let things happen as they should. Our first album, which a lot of people like, has a certain unity of mood. It has an intensity about it, because it was the first album we'd recorded. And we did it in a couple of weeks. That's all it took to get it down. It came after almost a year of almost total performance, every night. We were really fresh and intense and together.

This was at Elektra, of course. But you'd been signed to Columbia earlier. What happened there?

Well, it was just . . . in the beginning I'd written some songs and Ray [Manzarek] and his brothers had a band, Rick and the Ravens, and they had a contract with World-Pacific. They'd tried to get a couple of singles out and nothing happened. Well, they still had their contract to do a few more sides and we'd gotten together by then, and so we went in and cut six sides in about three hours. At that time, Robby wasn't with the group. But John [Densmore] was the drummer. Ray was on piano, I was singing and his two brothers . . . one played harp, one played guitar, and there was a girl bass player – I can't remember her name.

So what we got was an acetate demo, and we had three copies pressed, right? I took them around everywhere I could possibly think of . . . going to the record companies. I hit most of them . . . just going in the door and telling the secretary what I wanted. Sometimes they'd say leave your number, and sometimes they'd let you in to talk to someone else. The reception game. At Columbia they became interested. The first person anyone meets when they come to Columbia is the head of talent research and development. Actually, the first person is his secretary. They liked it.

This was Billy James . . .

Yeah, and a girl named Joan Wilson was his secretary. She called me a few days later and said he'd like to talk to us. We got a contract with Columbia for six months, during which they were going to produce so many sides. Having that contract was kind of an incentive for us to stay together. It turned out that no one was interested in producing us at that time, though, so we asked to get out of the contract.

Before the six months had elapsed?

Yeah. We knew we were onto something, and we didn't want to get held to some kind of contract at the last moment. By now we'd realised Columbia wasn't where it was at as far we were concerned. It was kind of fortunate, really. We've had a good relationship with the company we're with now. They're good people to work with.

Well, how'd that come about . . . with Elektra?

Elektra at that time was very new to the rock field. . . . They had Love, and early Butterfield stuff. But Butterfield was still into blues, into the folk bag. Love was their first rock group and actually represented their first singles potential. They had been mainly an album label. After they signed Love, the president of the company heard us play at the Whisky. I think he told me once he didn't like it. The second or third night . . . he kept coming back, and finally everyone was convinced we'd be very successful. So he signed us up.

I've been told or I read somewhere that after the Columbia episode, you were somewhat reluctant to sign with anybody else.

I can't remember exactly. The people said that everyone in town was trying to sign us up, but it wasn't really true. In fact, Jac Holzman's may have been the only concrete offer we had. We may have made him come up with the best deal possible, but there *was* no question but what we weren't that much in demand.

You said the first LP went easily . . .

Fast. We started almost immediately, and some of the songs took only a few takes. We'd do several takes just to make sure we couldn't do a better one. It's also true that on the first album they don't want to spend as much. The group doesn't either, because the groups pay for the production of an album. That's part of the advance against royalties. You don't get any royalties until you've paid the cost of the record album. So the group and the record company weren't taking a chance on the cost. So for economic reasons and just because we were ready, it went very fast.

Subsequent albums have been harder?

Harder and cost a lot more. But that's the natural thing. When we make a million dollars on each album and hit singles come from those albums, we can afford it. It's not always the best way, though.

In your early biographies, it says your parents are dead – yet your family is really very much alive. Why the early story?

I just didn't want to involve them. It's easy enough to find out personal details if you really want them. When we're born we're all footprinted and so on. I guess I said my parents were dead as some kind of joke. I have a brother, too, but I haven't seen him in about a year. I don't see any of them. This is the most I've ever said about this.

Getting back to your film, then, there's some of the most incredible footage I've ever seen of an audience rushing a performer. What do you think in situations like that?

It's just a lot of fun [*Laughter*]. It actually looks a lot more exciting than it really is. Film compresses everything. It packs a lot of energy into a small . . . anytime you put a form on reality, it's going to look more intense. Truthfully, a lot of times it was very exciting, a lot of fun. I enjoy it or I wouldn't do it.

You said the other day that you like to get people up out of their seats, but not intentionally create a chaos situation . . .

It's never gotten out of control, actually. It's pretty playful, really. We have fun, the kids have fun, the cops have fun. It's kind of a weird triangle. We just think about going out to play good music. Sometimes I'll extend myself and work people up a little bit, but usually we're out there trying to make good music, and that's it.

What do you mean, you'll sometimes extend yourself . . . work the people up a bit?

Let's just say I was testing the bounds of reality. I was curious to see what would happen. That's all it was: just curiosity.

What did you do to test the bounds?
Just push a situation as far as it'll go.
And yet you don't feel at any time that things got out of control?
Never.
Even in your film . . . when it shows cops throwing kids back off the stage as fast as they're diving onto it? That doesn't represent some loss of control?

You have to look at it logically. If there were no cops there, would anybody try to get onstage? Because what are they going to do when they get there? When they get onstage, they're just very peaceful. They're not going to do anything. The only incentive to charge the stage is because there's a barrier. If there was no barrier, there'd be no incentive. That's the whole thing. I firmly believe that. No incentive, no charge. Action-reaction. Think of the free concerts in the parks. No action, no reaction. No stimulus, no response. It's interesting, though, because the kids get a chance to test the cops. You see cops today, walking around with their guns and uniforms, and the cop is setting himself up like the toughest man on the block, and everyone's curious about exactly what would happen if you challenged him. What's he going to do? I think it's a good thing, because it gives the kids a chance to test the authority.

There are a number of cities where . . . like, you were busted for obscenity in New Haven. In Phoenix it was something else . . .

I would say in most cases the only time we get into trouble is, like, if a person is just walking down a busy street and for no reason at all just took their clothes off and kept on walking . . . you can do anything as long as it's in tune with the forces of the universe, nature, society, whatever. If it's in tune, if it's working, you can do anything. If for some reason you're on a different track from other people you're around, it's going to jangle everybody's sensibilities. And they're either going to walk away or put you down for it. So it's just a case of getting too far out for them, or everybody's on a different trip that night and nothing comes together. As long as everything's connecting and coming together, you can get away with murder.

There is a quote attributed to you. It appears in print a lot. It goes: 'I'm interested in anything about revolt, disorder, chaos . . .'

'. . . especially activity that appears to have no meaning.'

Right. That one. Is this another example of media manipulation? Did you make that one up for a newspaper guy?

Yes, definitely. But it's true, too. Who isn't fascinated with chaos? More than that, though, I am interested in activity that has no meaning, and all I mean by that is free activity. Play. Activity that has nothing in it except just what it is. No repercussions. No motivation. Free . . . activity. I think there should be a national carnival, much the same as Mardi Gras in Rio. There should be a week of national hilarity . . . a cessation of all work, all business, all discrimination, all authority. A week of total freedom. That'd be a start. Of course, the power structure wouldn't really alter. But someone offthe streets – I don't know how they'd pick him, at random perhaps – would become president. Someone else would become vice-president. Others would be senators, congressmen, on the Supreme Court, policemen. It would just last for a week and then go back to the way it was. I think we need it. Yeah. Something like that.

This may be insulting, but I have the feeling I'm being put on . . .

A little bit. But I don't know. People would have to be real for a week. And it might help the rest of the year. There would have to be some form or ritual to it. I think something like that is really needed.

There are a few words that recur in your dialogue. One is the word 'ritual'. What's that mean to you?

It's kind of like human sculpture. In a way it's like art, because it gives form to energy, and in a way it's a custom or a repetition, an habitually recurring plan or pageant that has meaning. It pervades everything. It's like a game.

Is there a ritual or a sense of game about what you and/or the Doors as a group do?

Yeah, it's a ritual in the sense that we use the same props and the same people and the same forms time after time after time. Music is definitely a ritual. But I don't think this is really clarifying ritual or adding anything to it.

Do you see yourself going more toward print?

That's my greatest hope. That's always been my dream.

Who turned you on to poetry?

I guess it was whoever taught me to speak, to talk. Really. I guess it was the first time I learned to talk. Up until the advent of language, it was touch – non-verbal communication.

What do you think of journalists?

I could be a journalist. I think the interview is the new art form. I think the self-interview is the essence of creativity. Asking yourself questions and trying to find answers. The writer is just answering a series of unuttered questions.

You've twice said you think you successfully manipulated the press. How much of this interview was manipulated?

You can't ever get around the fact that what you say could possibly turn up in print sometime, so you have that in the back of your mind. I've tried to forget it.

Is there some other area you'd like to get into?

How about . . . feel like discussing alcohol? Just a short dialogue. No long rap. Alcohol as opposed to drugs?

Okay. Part of the mythology has you playing the role of a heavy juicer.

On a very basic level, I love drinking. But I can't see drinking just milk or water or Coca-Cola. It just ruins it for me. You have to have wine or beer to complete a meal *[Long pause]*.

That's all you want to say? [Laughter]

Getting drunk . . . you're in complete control up to a point. It's your choice, every time you take a sip. You have a lot of small choices. It's like . . . I guess it's the difference between suicide and slow capitulation. . . .

What's that mean?

I don't know, man. Let's go next door and get a drink.

Z I G Z A G
John Tobler

Autumn 1970

John Tobler, one of Britain's most prolific rock writers,
interviewed Jim at the Isle of Wight Festival.
This was the Doors' second visit to England, taken
during a break in the Miami trial. The interview
is one of the briefest in the present collection, yet it
clearly shows the doubts that Jim held regarding any
talk about 'revolution' in America.

JOHN TOBLER: *I've discovered a book on sale at this festival called* The Doors Song Book, *which appears to be a pirated version of all the words off all the albums, including the new one. What do you reckon about that?*

JIM MORRISON: Well, I don't mind if they've got all the words spelt right. A lot of the time they really screw up the meaning, just one word or one semi-colon can ruin the whole thing.

Do you approve of having the lyrics on the back of your album or on the inside sleeve, because in England, two of them have had the lyrics and three haven't. Do you think it makes a difference? We didn't have the words to 'The Unknown Soldier' for instance.

Yeah, they really got botched up. I don't think it matters. I don't think it's necessary but . . .

You don't mind that somebody's making some bread out of your words?

No, what harm could it do?

Is this the first festival of this sort you've played?

Yes, it is.

How do you find it? I mean the chaos and the devastation and the . . . you know, it's OK in here, but have you been outside?

Well, it's kind of hard walking around out there. I did get around back around the camp-sites a little bit, but this one seems to be pretty well organised for such a huge event. I didn't have such a good time last night, because I had to perform, and I'd just gotten off the plane. But tonight, I came back, and I can see why people like it. I think all these people who say that huge festivals are over and dead, I think they're wrong. I think they're going to become increasingly significant in the next three or four or five years.

When I talked to some cats who came back from Woodstock, like Clive Selwood [London's Elektra representative], he said it was terrible. You know, the sheer inability to cope with the multitudes, and now they've made the film, and everyone's saying 'Wow! Beautiful revolution'.

I'm sure that these things get highly romanticised but I was kind of that opinion myself when I saw the film. It seemed like a bunch of young parasites, being kind of spoonfed this three or four days of . . . well you know what I mean. They looked like victims and dupes of a culture, rather than anything, but I think that may have been sour grapes, because I wasn't there, not even as a spectator, so I think that even though they are a mess, and even though they are not what they pretend to be, some free celebration of a young culture, it's still better than nothing. And I'm sure that some of the people take away a kind of myth back to the city with them, and it'll affect them.

I take it that you don't believe in this sudden, miraculous revolution that's being spoken about as if we're all going to go back to London and take over.

That would be unreal to me. I don't want to say too much because I haven't studied politics that much, really. It just seems that you have to be in a constant state of revolution, or you're dead. There always has to be a revolution, it has to be a constant thing, not something that's going to change things, and that's it, you know, the revolution's going to solve everything. It has to be every day.

I figure that you've got to convince people gradually to change, not to say 'Pow, we're coming in!' like the Black Panthers.

There have to be Black Panthers too. They have to change too, to become leopards some day, right?

You played mostly tracks off your first two albums last night. Why was that, because you thought we'd know those better?

No, we knew them better.

You don't do many gigs at that rate then?

Yeah, we do, but never anything like this. I don't think that our particular music style holds up very well in a huge outdoor event. I think that the particular kind of magic that we can breed when we do, when it works, works best in a small theatre.

Like the last time you came to England?

Yeah, that was beautiful, I think.

Yeah, right, I saw the last set; you know, when the dawn was breaking on the Saturday, and it was incredible.

I think that was one of the best concerts we've ever done.

I was talking to the guy this morning who made the film, and I said –
Which one?

Geoffrey Canon – he's a writer for The Guardian *– and he said that they were trying to put over the immediacy of rock, rather than the Doors, and I said well, I think you should have been trying to put over the Doors, because the sound recording was really shitty, you know.*

However, I thought the film was very exciting. To get it on national television, I think that's incredible. The thing is, the guys that made the film had a thesis of what their film was going to be, before we even came over. We were going to be the political rock group, and it gave them the chance to whip out some of their anti-American sentiments, which they thought we were going to give

233

them, and so they had their whole film before we came over. But I still think they made a very exciting film.

You know, when you were at the Roundhouse, there was something . . . It was amazing, all those people sitting there. It was so crowded it was much worse than this, because it was an enclosed space, and there was a queue of two thousand people waiting to get in at two o'clock in the morning. A ridiculous scene. Why haven't you been here since then?

I guess we've been too busy, and actually, there didn't seem to be that much demand. I mean, we couldn't go back to the Roundhouse; it would have to be a step forward, and there didn't seem to be any real, uh . . .

No. Well, the Roundhouse is no longer an auditorium in the same way. Oh Calcutta's on there, right?

Right.

That seems strange.

They put sort of terraced seating in not long after you came.

Well, that was a beautiful scene two years ago, at the Roundhouse where it's kind of a penny theatre, you know.

Right . . . It's the kind of thing one remembers for years and years, which is why I'd have expected an earlier return.

That's the reason. We were busy, and also there just didn't seem to be any real demand for it. What's the name of the magazine you guys put out?

Zigzag.

I've seen it. I'd like to start a magazine, newspaper thing in L.A. sometime. The trouble is, if you try and do it to sell copies, and get the advertising and all that, then you can't, uh . . .

Well, you certainly lose a lot of your enthusiasm when you start getting involved in business hustles. Anyway, wouldn't L.A. be rather a difficult market, with so many publications?

Well, that's it. I would only do it if I could finance it myself, so I wouldn't have to advertise. You know those little magazines, one issue things, the Surrealists and Dadaists used to put out? Manifestos, and all that?

Yeah, right.

Hey look. An actual movie. [*As Jimi Hendrix is filmed going up the backstage ramp followed by a man struggling with an enormous camera.*] Hey that's beautiful. Looks like a priest.

Do you think in view of what you've done that you will do a tour now?

Well, we had planned one . . . we had planned to do it after this, eight or nine places in Europe, including Italy and Switzerland and Paris, places like that, but I have to go back to this trial in

Miami. I'm in the middle of that, so it blew the whole trip.

That is such a drag, as far as we here are concerned.

I thought it was going to be, but it's actually a very fascinating thing to go through. A thing you can observe.

I talked to Jac Holzman [of Elektra], and he said that it was going on so long now that perhaps nothing would ever be done about it, because it would go to appeals and appeals and appeals, but the trouble is if it keeps you in a position where you can't get out of the country for too long, it's a drag for us here.

I think maybe we'll come back next Spring, March, April. That's a good time of year.

That would be good. Are you happy with the live album?

Yeah, I like it.

We haven't heard it yet.

It's just about to be released here. I think it's a true document of one of our good concerts. It's not insanely good, but it's a true portrait of what we usually do on a good night. I think you'll like it.

Well, I've really dug all the others. I heard that your favourite album was The Soft Parade. *Is that right?*

Oh, I don't know. I guess I don't have a favourite. Well, let's see, I think my favourite, beside the live one, is *Morrison Hotel*.

That's very good. That was getting back to the first two, perhaps, it seemed to me. Was that . . .

Just in the respect that we didn't use any other musicians on it, except the bass player.

Lonnie Mack –

But it wasn't a conscious attempt to get back to anything.

No, but it was publicised a bit like that here, which is perhaps unfair, because the first album is an epic. I'm literally on my third copy of it, I wore out two.

Yeah? You know, that's terrible, that's like a novelist's first novel, and no one ever lets him forget it. Why don't you write 'em like *Look Homeward Angel* anymore?

No, you're certainly progressing, aren't you? I mean, I thought Morrison Hotel *was a knock out, whereas* The Soft Parade *disappointed me in places.*

It kinda got out of control, and it took too long in making, spread over about nine months, and just got out of hand. There was no, uh . . . an album should be like a book of stories strung together, some kind of unified feeling and style about it, and that's what that one lacks.

Are you happy with Elektra?

Yeah, it's been a great relationship.

I'm an Elektra freak. I've got about seventy Elektra albums.

Well, now that it's become part of a large corperation, it'll be interesting to see if the label gets better, or if they kinda get . . . or if it gets assimilated. Hopefully, it might give them the chance not to worry about the tedium of the popular field, and do the thing that they do best, which is classical, experimental electronic things, giving a chance to people that haven't had really a chance to be commercially successful in their own times. Maybe this will give them a chance to get back to that.

Which is what they first became known for.

I think with us it was just really a freak. They've never repeated that.

Jac Holzman saw you when he went to see Love playing somewhere, didn't he? That was the story.

Right. They had Love, and someone associated with them brought someone in to see us, and that's . . . yeah, that's actually it. Because Love was the popular underground group in L.A. at that time, and we figured, well, if they went on Elektra, it must be a good label.

And then you got famous, and Love didn't.

Yeah. In a way that's true. I think it was sad about Love, they were incredible . . . well, it's really Arthur Lee, I suppose because . . . although the first Love group was a very, very great group. But I don't think they were willing to travel, and to go through all the games and numbers that you have to do to get it out to a large number of people. If they'd done that, I think they could have been as big as anyone. And someday they will.

Right. Thanks very much for your time.

Good luck.

C I R C U S
Salli Stevenson
Winter 1970

Salli Stevenson was a freelance writer in Los Angeles
when she met Jim in October, between the Miami trial
and sentencing, when he was living temporarily in the
Hyatt House Hotel on the Sunset Strip, sharing a suite
of rooms with his pal Babe Hill. The interview was
conducted on October 14th, transcribed the next day,
and given to Jim on the 16th for editing; he removed
some references to the trial which might have been
considered legally damaging should he be found guilty
and subsequently filed an appeal. Salli remembers the
interview, conducted at the Doors' office, as being 'very
businesslike until we got to the Phone Booth'. After that
it was 'outrageous', she says, but by then the tape
recorder had been put away.
The interview appeared in two instalments, in
December 1970 and January 1971,
in *Circus* magazine.

The Lizard King

PART I

No matter what your individual concept of hell is, it is always a comforting thought to enter, if indeed you must, in the company of friends who may on a lucky chance, James Bond-like, pull you out at that last desperate second before the master engulfs your spirit forever. Hell: how do you visualise it? The very concept of its corporality is elusive, fascinating and as frightening as the ruler of its dominions. The physical entity has come down to us on canvases too numerous to mention, all exploding fire and brimstone, revolt and desolation. Its potentate flashes across the medieval consciousness of our minds with cloven hooves, horns and a pitchfork, the better to roast us as so many marshmallows over the hot coals of what later centuries have suggested is our own paranoia.

That was the image we poor puritans were blessed with. Satan was our boogeyman, used to scare nasty children on dark nights and then . . . he became fashionable, a spirit to be glorified by public and press alike. The ultimate modish embodiment was personified in satanist Mick Jagger and demonic Jim Morrison, the American sexist devil of the late sixties.

Of Jim's 'Image' nothing remains to be said, for prior releases, journalistic meanderings and performances have spelled it out in clinicalised, explicit reams. The fact that his latest escapade landed him asunder of the law last summer in Miami was something else.

It was almost four o'clock when Kurt Inghan (our photographer) and I met Risa, friend and PR girl, and sallied forth to see Jim for the first of what was to be roughly two days in the life of. The office, an ex-antique shop on Santa Monica Blvd., is California stucco browns and golds. The fact that it is perpetual dusk inside blinds you to the presence of a very quiet Jim, sans paunch, sitting in a corner behind a desk. His smile is slow, genial, more in his eyes and in view of the ringing phones and takin' care of business voices he suggests that we try taping in the garden which features a minute pool with four frying sized gold fish, a distinct change from the lizards and snakes you half expect. Risa inquires after the crocodile only to find that that particular pool resident is late, great and gone which delights me no end. Lizards are passable, but crocs don't do much for my frazzled stomach and we are all just a bit edgy about confronting the 'Image'. Jim asks for a cigarette explaining that he only smokes when nervous.

SALLI STEVENSON: *Your latest album has received some rather harsh criticism, not only because it was another live album among the many released, but because of the lack of polish attributed to it by many critics. How did it come about and why the seeming lack of practice?*

JIM MORRISON: The *Live* album was condensed from about 24 hours of taped concerts that we did over approximately a year's period of time, starting with the Aquarius Theater in August 1969. We thought we might have one that night. We did two sets, but when we listened to it in the studio we found that it didn't really add up to a very good album. It was a good evening, but on tape it didn't sound that good. So we recorded seven or eight other concerts and listened to all of it and cut it down. I think it's a fairly true document of what the band sounds like on a fairly good night. It's not the best we can do and it's certainly not the worst. It's a true document of an above average evening. I like 'The Celebration', though it's not a great version of that piece, but I'm glad we went ahead and put it out, because I doubt if we would have ever put it on a record otherwise because it's a couple of years old. We tried to do it at the time we were doing *Waiting For The Sun* and it just didn't seem to make it in the studio, so we used one piece out of it, 'Not To Touch The Earth'. If we hadn't put it on a live album, we would have just shelved it forever. I'm glad that we did it even in the imperfect form in which it exists. It's better than if we had never done it. As far as the lack of practice . . . I think most of it is pretty professional. There are a few cuts that were done for the first time on stage, that we really hadn't worked with that much, that have flaws in them . . . but I don't think it's significant. People don't realise how different playing live is from recording. You work for days to get an instrumental track and then work for hours to get a vocal. Of course in a live thing, it's just that one shot. Basically the music has gotten progressively better, tighter and more professional . . . more interesting.

How then do you explain what appears to be a decline in your musical inventiveness over the last year or so? When you first started out, you were the great revolutionary hope of America and now the group seems to have mellowed.

Three years ago, if you remember, there was a great renaissance of spirit and emotion tied up with revolutionary sentiment. When things didn't change overnight, I think people resented the fact that we were just still around doing good music.

What about the deaths of Janis and Jimi. They went through the same period . . .

241

I think that that great creative burst of energy that happened three or four years ago was hard to sustain for the sensitive artists. I guess they might be dissatisfied with anything except 'the heights'. When reality stops fulfilling their inner visions, they get depressed.

RISA: *How do you think you'll die?*

I hope at about age 120 with a sense of humour and a nice comfortable bed. I wouldn't want anybody around. I'd just want to drift quietly off, but I'm still holding out. I think it's very possible that science has a chance in our lifetime to conquer death.

There are many people who believe in reincarnation and spirits. If medical science were to do that, what would happen to their spirit world?

They'd just have to fend for themselves. Leave us poor immortals alone.

I take it you don't believe in Karma or reincarnation or the occult beliefs?

No, not really, but since I don't have anything else to replace it with, I listen to everything. I don't say no.

What do you believe in then?

We evolved from snakes and I used to see the universe as a mammoth peristaltic snake. I used to see all the people and objects and landscapes as little pictures on the facets of their skins. I think the peristaltic motion is the basic life movement and even your basic unicellular structures have this same motion. It's swallowing, digestion, the rhythms of sexual intercourse.

It's been said that you've been on a superstar, super-ego trip. Has this affected you or your friends, or your relations with the band?

That's a complex one. Obviously you don't really talk about those things with people. I don't think it was that bad. I never noticed it too much except when I read magazine articles, but living in a town like L.A. you don't notice those images. People here are pretty blasé about things like that.

How about the magazines?

Actually I've always liked the things I've read. Of course it was about me. Usually you are most interested in yourself and people that you know. But . . . they were concentrating on my progenitive organ too much and weren't paying attention to the fact that I was a fairly healthy young male specimen who also had other than your usual arms, legs, ribs, thorax, eyes . . . but a cerebellum . . . your completely equipped human being with the head, sensitivity, the full equipment.

KURT: *For a while there was a cycle in pop stardom where people looked up to pop stars for their answers, forgetting that pop stars are people too.*

Now they seem to have come from idols to heroes.

Using the definition that a hero is someone you can reach out to and an idol is someone unreachable, do you consider yourself an idol or a hero?

A hero is someone who rebels or seems to rebel against the facts of existence and seems to conquer them. Obviously that can only work at moments. It can't be a lasting thing. That's not saying that people shouldn't keep trying to rebel against the facts of existence. Someday, who knows, we might conquer death, disease and war.

What about you, though . . .

I think of myself as an intelligent, sensitive human being with the soul of a clown, which always forces me to blow it at the most important moments.

If you had it to do over?

I'm not denying that I've had a good time these last three or four years. I've met a lot of interesting people and seen things in a short space of time that I probably would not have run into in twenty years of living. I can't say that I regret it. If I had it to do over, I think I would have gone for the quiet, undemonstrative artist, plodding away in his own garden.

When you were at U.C.L.A., you were involved in theatre and with that background you joined a band. Have your visions for the band become a reality?

Initially, I didn't start out to be a member of a band. I wanted to make films, write plays, books. When I found myself in a band, I wanted to bring some of these ideas into it. We never did much with it, though . . . it would take a long volume of prose to answer that with any degree of candour or truth. So, I think you're going to have to wait until I can get to work and write down what I really feel about that. It's too deep to cover in this amount of time and I wouldn't even want to give a short answer, because that's the most interesting question of all. I'm already working on it really, between interviews.

I like interviews . . . it's similar to answering questions on a witness stand. It's that strange area where you try and pin down something that happened in the past and try honestly to remember what you were thinking about, what you were trying to do. It's a crucial mental exercise. An interview will often give you a chance to confront your mind with questions which to me is what art is all about. It's a form of self-interview in which you pose yourself questions and try to come up with a reasonable answer. An interview also gives you the chance to try and eliminate all of those space fillers. All they do is if you can't think of an accurate answer you just 'kind of, you know, ahh, what I mean'.

KURT: *But everybody does it.*

I know. But you should not. Doctors, lawyers, scientists, good writers usually do. You'll notice that their conversation is much less vague than what you run up against with other people. It may be full of obscurities of its own kind, but you should try to be explicit, accurate, to the point . . . no bullshit. I like the interview form and I think it's going to become an increasingly important art form. It has antecedants in the confession box, debating and cross examination. Once you say something, you can't really retract it. It's too late. It's a very existential moment.

KURT: *Have you seen Alice Cooper or the Stooges?*

I haven't heard them. I've just read a few things about them . . . sounds great. I like people that shake other people up and make them uncomfortable.

Speaking of being uncomfortable, what's happening with the trial?

I had a six week trial and it was very interesting. The felony rap was dismissed and I'm still stuck with the two misdemeanours which could add up to eight months in jail. I'm admitting the charge of public profanity, but I'm denying the exposure charge. We're going to appeal that for as long as it takes to get it dismissed. It may take another year or two, I think it was more of a political than a sexual scandal. They picked on the erotic aspect, because there would have been no political charge they could have brought against me. It was too amorphous.

I really think that it was a lifestyle that was on trial more than any specific incident. Anyway, I go back to court on October 30th. *[Editor's note: This interview was conducted a few days before the trial.]* At that time there will be a sentence directed. The maximum would be eight months and a fine. However, whatever the sentence would be, even if it were suspended and there was a probation of some kind, we would still go ahead and appeal the conviction. The public profanity misdemeanour could be very easily dismissed because the Supreme Court has recently ruled that in a theatrical performance, not just theatrical performances, but in most other situations, the first amendment guarantees freedom of expression. That conviction would automatically be held unconstitutional. On the exposure charge we're maintaining innocence. Since the prosecution didn't come up with any real proof, we'll just appeal it and take it to a higher court. So I wouldn't go to jail immediately . . . I don't think.

It was a very interesting trial. I'd never actually seen the judicial system in action, the progress of a trial from the first day to the last. Being the defendant I had to be there for every day and it was fascinating . . . very educational. I wouldn't have chosen to have gone through the experience, but while it was happening all I could do was watch.

PART II

Sitting, watching and waiting for a possible doom factor to happen with no way to halt it is a gut-wrenching, nerve-racking experience. Then the waiting was over, Jim Morrison faced Judge Murray Goodman in Miami.

'You are a person graced with a talent, admired by many of your peers. Man tends to imitate that which he admires and those gifted with the ability to lead and influence others should strive to bring out the best, and not the worst in his admirers.' With that speech, Judge Goodman meted out the sentence for profanity and indecent exposure. Jim received six months, almost the maximum, and his bail was raised from $5,000 to $50,000. He is appealing the charge which could take up to three years and if successful, it is certain that he will have to serve no time at all. If the appeal fails he will probably serve a maximum of two months.

I was quite relieved that I wasn't taken into the jail and booked. They could have done it easily. I feel quite free for the first time in a year and a half. We're going to fight the sentence until it is wiped clean off the records. The appeal motion will first have to go to the Circuit Court in Florida and if it doesn't pass muster there, it will go to the State Court and eventually to the Supreme Court. If they accept it, there will be a final decision then.

On what factors is the appeal to be based?

The judge's attitude seemed to be that he was trying to prosecute me to the limits of the law. That will be one of our appeals, that I didn't really receive a fair trial because of judicial prejudice. For example, he limited the defence witnesses to the exact number that the prosecution had and he would allow no evidence regarding the contemporary community standards as, for example, taking the jury to see Woodstock and Hair and other current movies and plays that were showing in Miami at the time. These were two examples of his rigidity and lack of fairness in our opinion. The big charge, which was indecent exposure, was not conclusively proven in six weeks of testimony. There were ten to twelve thousand people there at the performance and countless cameras. The prosecution was not able to come up with one picture, one photograph of exposure.

I understand that your attorney made a direct appeal for mercy to the bench at your sentence date. What was it, and in your opinion, did the judge take that into consideration?

Max stated that he'd known me for four or five years and that he knew me to be a good man who had contributed some important works to society and most likely would continue to contribute. He stated that the mode of expression used to communicate thoughts that I had at Miami, was common in today's context and that it wasn't of evil intent. As to the other charge, there was no proof. But it seemed that the judge had already decided what he was going to do. His mind was made up prior to Max's bench appeal.

What was the state of mind you had that got you into this whole Miami mess in the first place?

I think I was just fed up with the image that had been created around me, which I sometimes consciously, most of the time unconsciously cooperated with. It just got too much for me to really stomach and so I just put an end to it in one glorious evening. I guess what it boiled down to was that I told the audience that they were a bunch of fucking idiots to be members of an audience. What were they doing there anyway. The basic message was . . . realise that you're not really here to listen to a bunch of songs by some fairly good musicians. You're here for something else. Why not admit it and do something about it.

You did the Isle of Wight . . .

That was during the trial. I flew over from Miami, arrived in London and drove to a little airport, took a small plane to the Isle of Wight and then we drove right to the concert. By the time I went on, I don't think I'd had any sleep in 36 hours. I wasn't really quite at my best . . . my peak of physical condition. I don't think it would have mattered that much anyway. The performance during that period would probably have been about the same anyway.

What about the mildly negative attitudes of the British newspapers?

Let's put it this way. We were not the highlight of the festivities. We weren't shitty by any means. Everyone sat there and listened and applauded like an audience is supposed to do.

What will happen to the group should you end up serving a sentence?

You would have to ask them, but I would hope that since all three of them are excellent musicians, they would go on and create an instrumental sound of their own that didn't depend on lyrics. Until then, we have another album to do. We'll be rehearsing and starting to do that album. Then films have always fascinated me and I'll get into that as quickly as possible and I have another book I want to write.

Will you ever write one about the trial?

Maybe I'll write the story of that someday. It might make a good journalistic exercise. One thing that came out of the trial was that I had a chance to get out of L.A. for an extended period of time for the first time in five years. Florida's a beautiful place – unpolluted more or less. I even had a chance to go down to Nassau and learned how to scuba-dive.

I read somewhere that you and the rest of the group owned an island down there.

No, I wish I did because the Caribbean is one of the most beautiful places I've ever visited. The water is perfectly clear and the sand is pure white. The sand out here is brownish in hue and you can see multi-coloured grains, but the sand down there is pure white. It looks like white shells, sea shells, that were ground up very finely. I wish I did own an island down there. They still have land for sale.

KURT: *They have hurricanes too, don't they?*

Yes, it keeps you close to nature. There's a guaranteed calamity every year.

Calamities . . . what about the police?

Police are different in every town and country. Some of the greatest police, unless you get on the wrong side of them, are the English bobbies. They seem to me very civil, gentlemanly kind of cats. The cops in L.A. are different from cops in most towns. They are idealists and they are almost fanatical in believing in the rightness of their cause. They have a whole philosophy behind their tyranny. In most places the police are doing a job, but in L.A. I've noticed a real sense of righteousness about what they are doing which is scary. On the road they're not bad. I was busted once in New Haven, Connecticut. When you are travelling with a band they usually give you hassles, but we're a pretty sedate group, no dopers or sex maniacs or anything like that. So, we have not really run up against too much harrassment. Usually when I go to a strange town, I just stay in the hotel and look out the window anyway.

There have been a lot of different things happening in America. What do you think the outcome for the country will be with the climate as it is now?

I think that whatever happens, America is the arena right now. It's the centre of action and it will take strong, fluid people to survive in a climate like ours. I'm sure people will do it but I think for many people, espcially city dwellers, it's presently a state of constant, total paranoia. As I understand it, paranoia is an irrational fear. The problem is . . . what if the paranoia is real. Then, all you can do is cope with it second by second.

LOS ANGELES FREE PRESS

Bob Chorush

Spring 1971

This was another one of the last interviews Jim gave before leaving Los Angeles for France. In it, Jim talked freely with Bob Chorush – who succeeded John Carpenter at the *Los Angeles Free Press* – about his court trials; the new Doors' album then being recorded, *L.A. Woman*; and a long list of other subjects, including theatre, film, poetry, reptiles, shamanism, and alcohol.

'There's no story really. No real narrative. Except there's a hitchhiker who . . . We don't see it, but we later assume that he stole a car and he drives into the city and it just ends there. He checks into a motel and he goes out to a nightclub or something. It just kind of ends like that.'

Jim Morrison is talking about the story of his latest movie HWY. *This amorphous plot summary seems strangely interchangeable with Morrison's new image of cinema verité director. The James Douglas Morrison that I spoke to several days ago was an older man than I had expected to meet. He was a man with grey hairs mingling into his beard and hair, talking about his past as a 'rock star' as a convict might review his past of 'criminal' with a parole officer. A sparkle of the Morrison that I had expected did at times come through, although the flashes were carefully obscured by the past tense.*

'It always amazes me that people think you're two years younger than you are. I guess that's why you have to keep doing interviews. People believe old press clippings. A couple of years ago, I filled a need that some people had for a figure who represented a whole lot of things, so they created the thing. It's like seeing baby pictures or something. It's embarrassing and funny at the same time.'

My preparation for talking to Morrison included reading three of his books (The Lords, The New Creatures *and* An American Prayer), *a* Rolling Stone *interview with him and press clippings dating back exactly four years. I was prepared to meet an alcoholic, drug crazed, megalomaniacal, slur-speeched, exhibitionist, rock star, film-maker in snakeskin pants and leather shirt, carrying a celebrated lizard under his arm. The first press statement that Morrison made laid the groundwork for my misconceptions.*

'You could say it's an accident that I was ideally suited for the work I am doing. It's the feeling of a bow string being pulled back for 22 years and suddenly being let go . . . I've always been attracted to ideas that were about revolt against authority. When you make your peace with authority you become an authority. I like ideas about the breaking away or overthrowing of established order. I am interested in anything about revolt, disorder, chaos, especially activity that seems to have no meaning. It seems to me to be the road towards freedom – external freedom is a way to bring about internal freedom.

'We are from the West. The whole thing should be like an invitation to the West. The sunset. The night. The sea. This is the end. Anything that would promote that image would be useful. The world we suggest should be of a new Wild West. A sensuous evil world. Strange and haunting, the path of the sun . . .'

Morrison is not the image that he has been for so many years. He isn't wearing snakeskin or leather. He has a beer with lunch and a drink before and after. He is his own archer's arrow travelling through the time and space of oblivion with a great deal of insight as to where he's been, and an Indian's aim of where he's going. He is more anxious to talk about films than rock music, a lot of which he no longer listens to. He is also anxious to get the details of his life straight; the most recent of which were his trials on charges ranging from obscenity to plane hijacking. Along with getting straight is the realization that with age, trials and tribulations, has come a loss of naivety.

JIM MORRISON: I wasted a lot of time and energy with the Miami trial. About a year and a half. But I guess it was a valuable experience because before the trial I had a very unrealistic schoolboy attitude about the American judicial system. My eyes have been opened up a bit. There were guys down there, black guys, that would go on each day before I went on. It took about five minutes and they would get 20 or 25 years in jail. If I hadn't had unlimited funds to continue fighting my case, I'd be in jail right now for three years. It's just if you have money you generally don't go to jail. The trial in Miami broke up a lot of things. It's on appeal to the Supreme Court right now.

BOB CHORUSH: *Whatever happened to the other busts that you were involved in?*

I got acquitted on everything else. We're trying to get this erased because it's not good to have something like that on your record.

Are you still concerned with that kind of record?

It's just if something really serious happens then you have a record and it looks a lot worse.

It looked for a while like they were out to get you. There was a federal hijacking charge also, wasn't there?

Well it came under a law that was created because of hijacking, but it wasn't really a hijacking. It was just a little over-exuberant kind of playing. It wasn't a threat to safety or anything. Actually we were acquitted because the stewardesses mistook me for someone who I was with. They were going by the seat number. They were saying that the person in such and such a seat was causing all this trouble. Then they all identified me as being in this seat. They were just trying to hang me because I was the only one that had a well-known face. So they were trying to get me for it. I don't know, I guess it was an example of the kind of people you meet on airplanes.

The trouble with all these busts is that people I know, friends of mine, think it's funny and they like to believe it's true and they accept it; people that don't like me like to believe it because I'm the reincarnation of everything they consider evil. I get hung both ways. I went through a trial there in Phoenix. I had to go back several times to get that cleared up.

What do you think the chances are of getting off in Miami? It's just a misdemeanour now isn't it?

Well, it's two misdemeanours. I have to be optimistic, so I figure there's a good chance. We're going to appeal on several grounds. First of all they never really proved anything except profanity, which we admitted all along. We were going to attempt to prove that profanity did not violate contemporary community standards in the City of Miami. To do that we were going to take the jury to see all the movies like *Woodstock* and *Hair*. *Hair* was playing in town at that time and they had nudity on stage every night and they were allowing young people to go in at any age. And even books that were available in Junior High School libraries had four-letter words. The judge refused to allow any investigation along those lines and limited it to criminal actions. They brought out thirteen witnesses. Every witness was either a policeman who was working there that night or someone who worked for the city and happened to be there, or a relative of a policman. In fact, their biggest witness was a sixteen-year-old girl who was the niece of a police officer who got her and her date in free on that night. All their testimony was very contradictory. Every one of them had a different version of what happened.

I heard that girl called someone 'a little bitch'.

I didn't hear her do it but that's what I heard. They had thousands of photographs from many different people that were there, but there was no photograph of an exposure or anything near it.

The other charges I think were just put in there to make it look more serious. Simulated masturbation, oral copulation . . .

With yourself?

Masturbation on myself and oral copulation on the guitar player. There's a picture of that on the inside sleeve of the *13* album.

Is that a lamb's head you're holding there?

No, that's a real lamb. That guy, Lewis Marvin of the Moonfire, happened to be there. He travels around spreading his philosophy of non-violence and vegetarianism. He carries this lamb around to demonstrate his principles that if you eat meat you're killing this little lamb. He gave it to me during the middle of the show. I just held it for a while. It's interesting. There was a lot of noise, a lot of commotion. It was almost deafening but the lamb was breathing normally, almost purring like a kitten. It was completely relaxed. I guess what they say about lambs to the slaughter is true. They don't feel a thing. Anyway, the judge limited the defence's witnesses to the number of witnesses that the prosecution brought on, which is an entirely arbitrary manoeuvre.

Did you get all those witnesses through an ad?

Yeah, and just through the grapevine. But we had over three hundred people that were willing to testify that they didn't see any of those alleged incidents. What it turns out actually happened is that a journalist happened to be there or heard about this concert and wrote a sensational front page story about the concert, about inciting to riot. The citizens became irate and began calling the police station asking why this had been allowed to go on and why I wasn't arrested. I had gotten up and gone on to Jamaica for a holiday that had been planned there. About three or four days after the whole thing, they swore out a warrant for me. So you can see how the whole thing began.

I spoke to Mike Gershman when he was down there with you and he said that you weren't able to perform during the whole course of the trial. Is it true that you were doing performances?

The only thing I did was the Isle of Wight for a day and then I came right back. We could have done performances but we never knew from one day to the next when court was in session.

They were doing alternate days, weren't they?

Yeah. And he changed it every day. So we never knew. I really needed the weekends to rest up. It was an ordeal.

Do you think they were out to get you or out to get the culture?

I think it was really the lifestyle they were going after. I don't think it was me personally. I just kind of stepped into a hornet's nest. I had no idea that the sentiment down there was so tender. The audience that was there seemed to enjoy it. I think that the people who read about it in the paper in this distorted version created a climate of hysteria. A few weeks later they had an anti-decency, I mean an anti-indecency, rally at the Orange Bowl with a famous fat comedian.

Well known for his decency.

Right. The President congratulated the kid that started this rally. They had them all over the country.

Did you find yourself excluded from the proceedings the way Manson feels.

Yeah. I felt like a spectator but I wouldn't have wanted to defend myself because I would have blown it, I'm sure. It's not as easy as it looks.

Did you ever get to testify at all?

Yes. I didn't have to testify, but we decided that it might be a good thing for the jury to see what I was like because all they could do is look at me for six weeks or as long as it went. So I testified a couple of days. I don't think it meant anything one way or another. They drag it out so long that after a while no one could care. I suppose that's one of the functions of a trial. They muddle it up so much that you don't know what to think anymore. That's society's way of assimilating a horrible event.

After clearing things up to the present, Morrison seems to feel more at ease about talking about the past. Someone has told me that Morrison used to be close with the Company Theater in Los Angeles until the group did Children of the Kingdom. *This play is a study of the thoughts and backstage actions of a 'rock star'. The resemblance between the play's protagonist and Morrison seems to be more than just mere coincidence. The protagonist, like Morrison, tried to realise what was going on in the heads of those that came to see him. Morrison's sense of theatrics had put him in front of a Los Angeles capacity audience reportedly asking 'What do you want? You didn't come here to hear music. What do you want? What do you REALLY want?'*

I saw half of *Children of the Kingdom*. I couldn't sit through the rest of it. It made me feel uneasy. Not that I don't appreciate a satire, but it just hit too close to home.

I think people go to rock concerts because they enjoy being in crowds. It gives them a feeling of power and security in a strange way. They like to rub up against hundreds of other people that are like them. It reinforces their trip.

As a performer then, I'm just a focus for everyone's attention, because you have to have an excuse to mob together. Otherwise it becomes a riot.

The Doors never really had any riots. I did try and create something a few times just because I'd always heard about riots at concerts and I mean I thought we ought to have a riot. Everyone else did. So I tried to stimulate a few little riots, you know, and after a few times I realised it's such a joke. It doesn't lead anywhere. You know what, soon it got to the point where people didn't think it was a successful concert unless everybody jumped up and ran around a bit. It's a joke because it leads nowhere. I think it would be better to do a concert and just keep all that feeling submerged so that when everyone left they'd take that energy out on the streets and back home with them. Rather than just spend it uselessly in a little crowd explosion.

No, we never had any real riots. I mean a riot's an out of control, violent thing. We never had too much of what I call a real riot. I think also it has something to do with swarming theory. The idea that when the population starts outstripping the food supply, animals or insects swarm together. It's a way of communicating. Working out a solution or signalling awareness to each other. Signalling that there is a danger. In nature a balance is worked out and I think that somehow that's what's happening. In Los Angeles or New York and many of the big cities, you feel crowded. You feel psychologically crowded and physically crowded. People are getting very neurotic and paranoid and I guess things like rock concerts are a form of human swarming to communicate this uneasiness about overpopulation. I haven't really got it all worked out yet but I think there's something in it.

I think that more than writing music and as a singer, that my greatest talent is that I had an instinctive knack of self-image propagation. I was very good at manipulating publicity with a few little phrases like 'erotic politics'. Having grown up on television and mass magazines, I knew instinctively what people would catch on to. So I dropped those little jewels here and there – seemingly very innocently – of course just calling signals.

I think the Doors were very timely. The music and ideas were very timely. They seem naive now, but a couple of years ago people were into some very weird things. There was a high energy level and you could say things like we did and almost half-ass believe them. Whereas now it seems very naive. I think it was a combination of good musicianship and timeliness. And we may have been one of the first groups to come along who were openly self-conscious of being performers and it was reflected in our career as it was happening.

It's not that we were trend conscious or anything like that. We were doing exactly what we would have been doing anyway. It came at the right time and we could get away with expressing sentiments like that. I'm sure we would have done the same thing anyhow. For example, the first album is not really socially conscious, it's just very universal personal statements. Each album got a little more socially aware of the whole landscape, perhaps to the detriment of the music.

As we travelled and played to large groups of people, then some of the words couldn't help reflecting the things I ran into. That was mainly it. It wasn't any conscious programme. Probably the things we record now will get back to the blues. That's what we do best. We may even do a couple of old blues songs. Just your basic blues.

It'll be good blues. It won't be like a guy with a guitar playing the blues. It will be electric blues, I hope. You never know when you start an album, it could be entirely different. But that's what I'm going to push for. That's the music I enjoy best. It's the most fun to sing. I like jazz too. But you don't need a singer really for jazz. Those guys ought to do some instrumentals. I've always pushed for that. They've been reluctant to do it but I wish they would. Those guys put out a lot of music, a lot of sound for just three guys.

I like any reaction I can get with my music. Just anything to get people to think. I mean if you can get a whole room or a whole club full of drunk, stoned people to actually wake up and think, you're doing something. That's not what they came there for. They came to lose themselves.

I don't know if you saw the set up we have at the office or not. We have a board upstairs. We record right there. It's not that we don't like the Elektra studios, but we felt that we do a lot better when we're rehearsing. We leave a tape running. It's a lot cheaper and faster that way too. This will be the first record that we're actually doing without a producer. We're using the same engineer that we've used, Bruce Botnick. I don't know if he'll be called a producer or not. Probably co-producer with the Doors. In the past, the producer . . . it's not that he was a bad influence or anything, but this will be a lot different without that fifth person there. So anyway, we'll be by ourselves for better or worse.

There were a few new songs on the *Live* album. A year ago we finished *Morrison Hotel*. It's been about a year since we've been in a studio.

A few years ago I wanted to do live performances. I was trying to get everyone to do free surprise spots at the Whisky but no one wanted to. Now everyone wants to, and I totally lost interest. Although I know it's a lot of fun, I just don't have the desire to get up and sing right now. I still enjoy music, but I lost a lot of interest in it.

Are you going to go in more for doing your films?

Yeah, I think so, but there's no hurry on that.

You've done about five films, haven't you?

HWY is the only real film I did. I was involved in the other ones but they weren't totally my films. *HWY* is, to a large degree. I only see films as a team effort except in a few rare cases. I'd like to get *HWY* shown. I think maybe it might work on educational television. N.E.T. It's about the right length. You see, it's an uncommercial type film. It's too long for a short play with another feature and it's not a feature itself. It's fifty minutes, an awkward length but I think maybe educational TV might be a good spot for it.

I was always fascinated with a story about a hitchhiker who becomes a mass murderer. I set out to make that film but it turned into a different film. A much more subtle fantasy. Someday, I'd still like to make that hitchhiker film. 'Cause I think it's a good one.

You played the hitchhiker in HWY. *Is acting something you want to get into?*

No, it was just easier that way.

A couple of things that you said about The Lords *interested me, like 'the appeal of cinema lies in the fear of death'. Is that something you can explain?*

I think in art, but especially in films, people are trying to confirm their own existences. Somehow things seem more real if they can be photographed and you can create a semblance of life on the screen. But those little aphorisms that make up most of *The Lords* – if I could have said it any other way I would have. They tend to be mulled over. I take a few seriously. I did most of that book when I was at the film school at U.C.L.A. It was really a thesis on film aesthetics. I wasn't able to make films then, so all I was able to do was think about them and write about them and it probably reflects a lot of that. A lot of the passages in it, for example about shamanism, turned out to be very prophetic several years later because I had no idea when I was writing that I'd be doing just that.

At the end of The Lords, *you define the Lords as the people that are controlling art. Did I understand that right?*

Strangely enough, that's what I meant. Not controlling art necessarily. What that book is a lot about is the feeling of powerlessness and helplessness that people have in the face of reality. They have no real control over events or their own lives. Something is controlling them. The closest they ever get is the television set. In creating this idea of the Lords, it also came to reverse itself. Now to me the Lords mean something entirely different. I couldn't really explain. It's like the opposite. Somehow the Lords are a romantic race of people who have found a way to control their environment and their own lives. They're somehow different from other people.

Is there a particular person you could think of . . .?

No, it's not about any particular person.

I wanted to talk a bit about your poetry also.

Sure, go right ahead.

The New Creatures. *There's a lot of creatures in everything you do. Lizards and snakes and snakeskins. That's part of your reputation. 'The Lizard King'. How did all that come about?*

I had a book on lizards and snakes and reptiles and the first sentence of it struck me acutely – 'reptiles are the interesting descendants of magnificent ancestors'. Another thing about them is that they are a complete anachronism. If every reptile in the world were to disappear tomorrow, it wouldn't really change the balance of nature one bit. They are a completely arbitrary species. I think that maybe they might, if any creature could, survive another world war or some kind of total poisoning of the planet. I think that somehow reptiles could find a way to avoid it.

Does that fit into your own self-concept?

Also, we must not forget that the lizard and the snake are identified with the unconscious and with the forces of evil. That piece 'Celebration of the Lizard' was kind of an invitation to the dark forces. It's all done tongue-in-cheek. I don't think people realise that. It's not to be taken seriously. It's like if you play the villain in a Western it doesn't mean that that's you. That's just an aspect that you keep for show. I don't really take that seriously. That's supposed to be *ironic*.

On a much more basic level, I just always loved reptiles. I grew up in the South-West and I used to catch horned toads and lizards. Of course I still can't get too close to snakes. I mean it's hard for me to pick up a snake and play with it. There's something deep in the human memory that responds strongly to snakes. Even if you've never seen one. I think that a snake just embodies everything that we fear. Basically their skins are just beautiful. I guess that's why they're so fashionable. I think they always have been.

There's probably also a little victory in taking the snake and wearing it.

Yeah, sure. What do they call it – a totem. No, not a totem, a talisman. When I wrote *The New Creatures*, I was very naive. It wasn't something that was born out of any great awareness of the universe. It's a very naive little book, but somehow a lot of it holds up.

Do you think you'll be able to do as well on film as you did with the Doors?

I don't see why not. I get an instinctive feeling for the film media. I think I'll do pretty well at it.

I've noticed that when someone puts down a good film the best reaction you can get if it's of the same intensity as a Doors concert is that people walk out on it.

Well, see, I like that kind of thing. I've never thought that an audience should be as passive as they've become. I think that an audience should be an active participant in creating what's happening. You can even do that with a film. For example, it's up to you to close your eyes anytime you want or get up and walk out for five minutes. That makes it an entirely different movie than what a person would see if he sat dutifully through it from beginning to end, right?

Did you try to do a live performance as part of Feast of Friends *in San Francisco?*

Did we show that up there? I think we may have at one time. We showed it at the Aquarius after the concert was over, but that doesn't mean anything. That was just because we'd made this film and we felt it was really good and no one would distribute it. So we just show it when we can. I'm glad we made it. It will be a good document of that era.

Do you feel that people are more willing to accept your films or more willing to reject them knowing your notoriety or your background as a singer?

I think that I may get a chance to do a film because of that notoriety. I'll probably get *one* chance. If it doesn't really make it, it will probably be very hard to get another chance. But I think that almost anyone can get one chance nowadays to make some kind of film.

Do you find that your reputation as 'rock singer' gets in the way?

They always want a soundtrack or they even have the audacity to want you to play a singer for the movie. I'm not really interested in acting. It doesn't bother me that much.

What's your reputation as a drinker?

[*Long pause*] I went through a period where I drank a lot. I had a lot of pressures hanging over me that I couldn't cope with. I think also that drinking is a way to cope with living in a crowded environment, and also a product of boredom. I know people drink because they're bored. I enjoy drinking. It loosens people up and stimulates conversation sometimes. It's like gambling somehow, you go out for a night of drinking and you don't know where you're going to end up the next day. It could work out good or it could be disastrous. It's like the throw of the dice.

There seem to be a lot of people shooting smack and speed and all that now. Everybody smokes grass – I guess you don't consider that a drug anymore. Three years ago there was a wave of hallucinogenics. I don't think anyone really has the strength to sustain those kicks forever. Then you go into narcotics, of which alcohol is one. Instead of trying to think more you try and kill thought with alcohol and heroin and downers. These are pain killers. I think that's what people have gotten into. Alcohol for me, because it's traditional. Also, I hate scoring. I hate the kind of sleazy sexual connotations of scoring from people so I never do that. That's why I like alcohol, you can go down to any corner store or bar and it's right across the table.

I think what happens now is that people smoke so much and so constantly that it's not a trip anymore. I think they build up a cellular tolerance for it. It just becomes part of their body chemistry. They're not really stoned.

Morrison talks on. Always conscious about his image. Relaxed. He is fascinated by a mini-skirted girl who gets out of a car across the street, and by Zap Comix. He wants to write about his trial and wonders where he should submit his story. He drops hints about a friend of his who could be the world's greatest female vocalist. He seems nervous about getting back to the studio. He's already two hours late. But . . .

There is no story really. No real narrative . . . he drives into the city . . . he goes out . . . or something . . . it just kind of ends like that . . . and . . . when the music's over, turn off the lights . . .

Jim Morrison's film career is about to begin.

ROLLING STONE

Ben Fong-Torres

Spring 1971

The Doors were recording their final album *L.A. Woman*, as a quartet, when one of *Rolling Stone*'s pre-eminent interviewers, Ben Fong-Torres, talked to them in Los Angeles. With the Miami trial finally behind him, Jim was now free to talk about it. The article was published in March 1971, shortly before Jim went to Paris.

The Lizard King

Los Angeles – Jim Morrison and the Doors are back home in Hollywood and at work on an album – this time without producer Paul Rothchild, and this time featuring 'blues', Morrison says, 'original blues, if there's such a thing'.

Morrison, the ex-sex symbol of West Coast rock; the poet who called himself 'Lizard King' is a convicted man, following a two month trial in Florida for his alleged organ recital at a March, 1969 concert in Miami. He was found guilty of misdemeanours – indecent exposure and open profanity – and his case is on appeal – probably for an indefinite time. He's out on bail.

Jim Morrison, all of the above, is still a Door. He continues the transition from rock'n'roll to poetry and films. And he has aged. His face is still jungular, but now more lion-like than Tarzanic, outlined as it is by comfortably long dark hair and full, dark beard. And he's got the beginning of a beer belly. Quiet about his Miami case in the Rolling Stone *interview he did in July 1969 and silent, still, during the trial, Morrison seemed eager to talk a bit when we ran into each other in Hollywood – to put the old days in proper perspective, to discuss the Doors, and to assess the whole Miami thing, in his own words.*

BEN FONG-TORRES: *Do you still consider yourself the 'Lizard King'?*

JIM MORRISON: That was two years ago, and even then it was kind of ironic. I meant it ironically . . . half tongue-in-cheek. It was an easy thing to pick up on. I just thought everyone knew it was ironic, but apparently they thought I was mad.

Do you think you'd be classified among the people who signify what some people insist is the 'death of rock'?

Well, I was saying rock is dead years ago. What rock means to me is – for example, in one period 20 or 30 years ago, jazz was the kind of music people went to, and large crowds danced to and moved around to. And then rock'n'roll replaced that, and then another generation came along and they called it rock. The new generation of kids will come along in a few years, swarm together, and have a new name for it. It'll be the kind of music that people like to go out and get it on to.

But back 20, 30 years ago the music didn't become a symbol of a whole new culture or subculture.

But, you know, each generation wants new symbols, new people, new names – they want to divorce themselves from the preceding generation; they won't call it rock . . . Don't you see a cyclical thing every five or ten years, when everyone comes together and swarms and breaks apart . . . When you think of rock, it's not mind music. I mean, if you couldn't understand the words, there'd still be everything there to react to.

How about Miami? Will that whole thing affect whether you'll play any more concerts?

I think that was the culmination, in a way, of our mass performing career. Subconsciously, I think I was trying to get across in that concert – I was trying to reduce it to absurdity, and it worked too well.

When did it stop getting to be fun?

I think there's a certain moment when you're right in time with your audience and then you both grow out of it and you both have to realise it; it's not that you've outgrown your audience; it has to go on to something else.

You see blues fitting in with this?

No, it's just getting back to more of what we enjoy. What we actually personally enjoy. Not that we've ever not played music that we didn't like. When we were playing clubs, I'd say over half of what we did was blues, and we used our own material on records, but I think the most exciting things we did were basic blues. I like them mainly 'cause they're fun to sing.

We're using Elvis' bass player – his name is Jerry, damn it, I forget his last name [Scheff] – and for the first time we recorded it in our office where we rehearse, and the board's upstairs; we're using the engineer that we used on the other records – Bruce Botnick – but we're not using Paul Rothchild on this one. It was kind of mutual; just figured it was time . . . to take different roads.

What was your main interest in the Miami case, aside from your personal liberty?

You know, I was hoping – or I thought there might be a possibility of it becoming a major, ground-breaking kind of case, but it didn't turn out that way. It might have been one of the reasons why they dragged it out so long in order not to let enough momentum or sentiment build up in a short time, or a lot of attention focus on it. So it actually received very little national attention. But in a way I was kind of relieved, because as the case wore on, there were no great ideals at stake.

I thought it might become just a basic American issue involving freedom of speech and the right of anyone with a personal view-point to state their ideas in public and receive a hearing with-out legal pressure being put on them. In fact my lawyer made a speech part way through the trial in which he traced the origin of freedom of speech which goes side by side with the origin of drama, actually. The right of the dramatist or artist to state his views. It was a brilliant summary of that historical process, but it didn't have any effect on the outcome at all. The first amendment provides sup-posedly for the freedom of expression. There's a clause which states that any dramatic or public artistic performance comes under this amendment.

Basically the prosecution refused to listen to any testimony which would come under that clause. They were prosecuting totally on a criminal case. My defence counsel was prepared to put the whole case on the fact that even if this alleged event did occur, it did not violate contemporary community standards, and they were going to take the jury to see *Woodstock*, a lot of other films – and during the trial the production company of *Hair* opened up in Miami, and they had obscenity and full nudity on stage in it, and there were no restrictions on it as to the age of the audience – they let anybody in – but the judge anticipated that, and he threw out the proceedings.

But is that a really relevant parallel? In Hair, *say, that profanity and that alleged obscenity is planned as part of the act. Would you then have to testify that whatever acts you took were part of your act? Yours were spon-taneous.*

But it is a theatrical performance, nonetheless. It's not a political rally. We go on to a series of songs that everyone's familiar with. The people who come to the shows have the albums and I think they know basically what they're coming to see.

I suppose they could've had a point there, but they never even got into that.

What did they find you guilty of?

There were four charges – one was a felony which carried a three year rap – for lascivious behaviour including exposure. And three misdemeanours – one was on profanity; one was on – let's see – oh, public drunkenness, and the other was one which included the exposure charge; it was a separate one. So constitutionally, right there they were wrong. You're not supposed to be able to try a per-son on the same count twice. You could argue that anyway. That's probably one of the motions that we'll include in the appeal.

Why wasn't that argued in the very beginning? Couldn't you have called for a dismissal of the trial?

266

Yeah, we called for a dismissal a score of times, but they were all denied.

Another cause for argument was that there was no possible way I could have received a fair trial because of the climate of public opinion that had been stirred up for a year and a half – probably a newspaper story or a radio or TV story in Miami. We have a sheaf of clippings that takes up two files from all over the country. But one thing I was interested to observe: every day we would rush home to watch ourselves on TV; they couldn't film in the court room, but going and leaving they'd film it, and we'd hear the reporters' views of what had happened. The first few days it was kinda the old-line policy, what people had been thinking for a year and a half, but as the trial wore on, the reporters themselves, from just talking to me and the people involved in the case – the tone of the news articles – and even the papers – became a little more objective as each day went on.

What's in the immediate future for the Doors? Any concerts?

No, we're kind of off playing concerts; somehow no one enjoys the big places anymore, and to go into clubs more than just a night every now and then is kind of meaningless. I think we'll do a couple of albums and then everyone will probably get into their own thing; each guy in the band has certain projects that they want to do more independently. I heard that Robbie would like one on his own, predominantly a guitar thing, and John has always been – basically he likes jazz, and I would suspect he might produce and play in a jazz album. Robbie and John a couple of years ago produced an album of some friends of theirs called *A Comfortable Chair*; they've both got an ear for producing.

How about yourself? Do you have a film project?

Ahhh . . . I guess that's what I've always wanted to do, even more than being in a band, was working in films. I'd like to write and direct a film of my own – there's one that's all in my head, but I have a film which I made, which hasn't been seen very much, it's called *HWY*.

Wasn't it shown up in Canada at a 'Jim Morrison Film Festival'? How did it go over?

The reports I got were that *HWY* was very enthusiastically received.

That wasn't the case in San Francisco at the film festival there . . .

Feast of Friends was shown there a year or so ago with a lot of boos. I think they were reacting to personalities rather than the film. *HWY* was entered in the San Francisco Film Festival, but it was

267

rejected, for whatever reason. It's a 50 minute film, 35 millimeter, and in colour. I act in it and made it with some friends of mine. It's more poetic, more of an exercise for me, kind of a warm up. There's no story in it. Just a hitchhiker who steals a car . . . we assume that, anyway . . . and he drives into town and checks into a motel or something and it just kind of ends like that.

LAST WORDS

IN THE SPRING of 1971, just months before he died, Jim hand-scrawled a letter to Dave Marsh, who was then the editor of *Creem* magazine. Jim used a lined notepad and his script was large, so that he wrote on every other line. Sometimes he would cross out words and phrases. His vocabulary was simple, the sentences taut and flat like Ernest Hemingway's. Marsh had asked about the new album then being recorded. Jim answered the question and then, typically, threw in some philosophy:

He started the letter off with a simple technical description of the making of the album – in their 'rehearsal studio w/an 8-track in the office upstairs', producing it themselves with Bruce Botnick as engineer and co-producer. There's a feeling of satisfaction, excitement even, in the straightforward statement that 'This is a blues album'.

'The songs have a lot to do w/ America & what it's like to live these years in L.A.,' he wrote, adding that he saw the city as a 'genetic blue-print' for the United States. He admitted in the letter that he had had the 'fortunate' chance to work out a personal myth there, a 'late adolescent phantasy [sic] on reality terms at large'. After mentioning *HWY* and other things that he was working on, including 'a long essay on the Trial in Florida', he signed off:

'I am not mad.
I am interested
in freedom.
Good luck.
J Morrison'

ACKNOWLEDGEMENTS

I would like to thank John Tobler for originally commissioning this book some years ago. Thanks to my publishers Sandra Wake and Terry Porter at Plexus Publishing for being instrumental in making it finally happen and to Nicky Adamson for her role as editor, midwife and mother. Without their unflagging effort and meticulous attention to detail the many loose ends would have remained untied forever.

I would also like to thank the writers, and editors, who contributed their Morrison interviews: Art Kunkin, Bob Chorush, the late John Carpenter, Salli Stevenson, Jerry Rothberg, John Tobler, Richard Goldstein, Ben Fong-Torres and Jann Wenner. Thanks also to the original publications: *Rolling Stone* magazine and Straight Arrow Publishers Inc, *Circus* magazine and Circus Enterprizes Corp, *Zigzag* magazine and the *Los Angeles Free Press*.

Acknowledgement for help with research and in assembling the interviews and visual material to: Jeannie Cromie, Diane Gardiner, Robert Klein, Art Kunkin, Rainer Moddemann, Hervé Muller, Patricia Keneally Morrison, Danny Sugerman, Dave Marsh, Stephen Adamson, Sandra Cowell, Harvey Weinig and Jann Wenner. And to Corinne Brinkman for translating the Paris documents concerning Morrison's death.

Finally grateful thanks to the following photographers: Joel Brodsky and Elektra Records for the cover photograph; Robert Klein pages 14, 42, 47, 50/51, 61, 62, 68, 83; Ed Caraeff pages 6, 13, 17, 52, 55, 58, 67, 79, 90, 126, 262; David Sygall pages 23, 27, 72, 210; Baron Wolman pages 24, 94, 107, 123; Mike Barich pages 2, 88/89, 107, 118, 261, 268; Gloria Stavers/Starfile/Pictorial Press pages 20, 31, 76; Raeanne Rubenstein/People in Pictures pages 28, 142; Joseph Sia pages 102, 109, 113, 153; Jeff Simon pages 131, 135; WEA/Elektra Records/Paul Ferrara page 188; WEA/Elektra Records/Edmund Teske page 216; WEA/Elektra Records/Jeff Simon page 248; Andrew Kent page 158; Claude Gassian pages 177, 185; Barry Plummer pages 201, 230; Don Paulsen page 8/9; UPI Bettmann Newsphotos page 101; the US Navy Public Information Office pages 35, 41; Araldo di Crollalanza pages 114, 202; Edmund Teske page 147; Hervé Muller pages 163, 166, 171; Jane Hopkins page 238; George Washington High School, Virginia page 38; Chris Walter page 65; Steen Kaersgaard page 98/99; Peter Saunders page 105; the Department of State Foreign Service of the United States of America page 175; Sounds page 237.

Jerry Hopkins, 1992